D0651559

The Pulse of Hope

A Surgeon's Memoirs from Poverty to Prosperity

William A. Reed

THE PULSE OF HOPE:
A SURGEON'S MEMOIRS FROM POVERTY TO PROSPERTY

www.thepulseofhope.com

Walsworth Publishing
Marceline, Missouri

ISBN 978-0-9907404-0-7

First Edition September 2014

PHOTOGRAPHY CREDITS

Reed Family Collection

Leeanne Seaver
seavercreative.com

Kokomo Public Schools

University of Kansas Medical Center

The *Kansas City Star* newspaper

Cover and book design by 94 Design
Marthasville, Missouri
94design.com

Library Of Congress Cataloging

Reed, William A.
    The Pulse of Hope: a surgeon's memoirs from poverty to prosperity/
    William A. Reed.-1stEd

*Dedicated to the memory
of my mother,
Aldine Caroline Reed,
for instilling within me
a sense of hope.*

Jay, Mother and Bill, 1942

William Reed's study at Stonecrest Farm, 2014

Author's Note

It is my prayer that this book might provide a bit of light during dark times for its reader. I hope it gives courage and optimism for life's adventure. To those who have helped me tell my story in so many ways, you have my sincere gratitude. For your time and thoughtful contributions, I would like to thank: LaDonna and Rick Allen, Bill Barkman, Jo Jeanne Callaway, Beth Davis, Bill Hamaker, Betty Keim, Lynn Kindred, Pat Kinsman, Michael McCloskey, Representative Steve Morris, Representative Kathy Wolfe Morris, Steve Owens, Bob Page, Henry Pearley, Tammy Peterman, Charles Porter, Greg Reed, Lucy Reed, Chris A. Ross, Elaine Russell, Garrett Smith, Irene Thompson, Pat Twenter, and William Wofford.

My very special thanks must be expressed to Jeff Kramer for his important contribution of the Foreword, as well as for his careful reading of early drafts of this book. Also, my profound gratitude goes to James Still for writing the beautiful Epilogue, and for reaching out to me fifty years after we originally touched one another's life. I'm indebted to both of you for your heartfelt support.

Credit for the idea to share my life story, and, ultimately, the decision to move forward with its writing goes to my friend and colleague Jill Jensen Chadwick, the media and public relations aficionado at the University of Kansas Medical Center. She believed in this project and subsequently introduced me to Leeanne Seaver, a talented writer and collaborator. Leeanne's ability to glean the essence of my life from our many discussions was remarkable. This book is built from our conversations about who I am as a heart surgeon, horseman, family man, part-time poet and philosopher. Our exploration of the miracle of nature and creation and the meaning of it all relative to my life's experience has been inspiring and enriching.

My love and gratitude to my family for their many contributions through this long and time-consuming process is vast. None of this would have been possible without your support and individual contributions at sensitive times. I'm eternally grateful to each of you: Jeff and Rita, Bryan and Dianne, and Martin.

To my wife, Mary, for sharing my life . . . the exciting, fulfilling times as well as the frustrating hard times . . . for all that we have shared and will continue to share, I thank you for your love, your support and your understanding.

William Reed

Contents

Foreword

"We make a living by what we get;

we make a life by what we give."

~ Sir Winston Churchill

William Reed's improbable story is almost unfathomable in our present day and age . . . given his background, the traditional formulas for success didn't apply here. Indeed, there is a lot more to know about Bill Reed, who is considered the Father of Cardiovascular Surgery in Kansas City. Yes, he was a pioneer, a builder of storied programs, a championship horse aficionado, and a philanthropist, but there is much, much more behind this image that explains this remarkable man and the times that shaped him.

Dr. Reed appeared on the medical scene when the nascent field of cardiac surgery was like the Wild West of medicine. Open-heart operations were unpredictable and death was never far away. It was an era of innovation—making it up as you went along—sometimes with every operation. They were tough times for the surgeon as well as the patient since "defeat" was a demoralizing possibility – a result of one's active intervention, no matter how good the intention. These defeats felled many a surgeon in those days—men who could not see beyond the present. What would the medical world be like today without Dr. Reed and the few colleagues who persisted?

What kind of man is driven to such heights of achievement? For starters, Dr. Reed is entirely self-made. Nothing was handed to this man, who grew up in abject poverty. Yes, he was fortunate to be born with exceptional intelligence and willpower, and blessed to have found the ideal life companion in his wife, Mary. Also, he was able to find colleagues who could help him along his journey. Yet what stands out in this memoir is how he looks at the world differently from most. William Reed derives his strength and motivation from service to others.

I have been one of those fortunate enough to have known Dr. Reed both on a professional and personal level over a few years now. Bill is not only the consummate surgeon, but a man of many dimensions; someone who can spontaneously discuss poetry and philosophy as well as the intricacies of aortic valve replacement. Our hours of conversation about life and all of the above have helped put things in perspective for me . . . and I suspect he has affected many others in this way, too.

Dr. Reed has foibles, doubts, weaknesses as we all do, and he freely admits them. Yet, his commitment to excellence, his true engagement with fellow human beings, his humility and understanding of our miniscule position in the universe set him apart, even from leaders of great stature in and outside the world of medicine.

This is a rare glimpse into the mind of someone who belongs to a grand generation, the likes of whom will not appear again.

Jeffrey B. Kramer, MD

Prologue

You have to carry the fire.

I don't know how to.

Yes, you do.

Is the fire real? The fire?

Yes it is.

Where is it? I don't know where it is.

Yes you do. It's inside you. It always was there. I can see it.

~ *Cormac McCarthy,* **The Road**

I don't know how many hearts I've put back together or replaced, well over ten thousand. If it ever occurred to me that my own might not be whole, I tried not to indulge the thought. Whatever gift I've been given to do this work has been grace enough to do it well, better than most, maybe even the best at times. I would never have said so myself, but others have. Whatever "the best" was, it was certainly the result of "we," not just "me."

It always gave me an unnamable feeling to gaze into the empty space where the sick, crippled heart I had just removed once sustained the life of the person lying on the operating table. And in my hands was the heart of someone else that we hoped would fill the void. When transplanting a heart, there is that moment, Eliot's "space between waves," when everyone in the OR along with everyone in the waiting room and everyone sitting by their phone in homes or offices somewhere else in the world waiting for word willed all of life's possibilities into that first tentative beat . . . and then another one, steadier.

Who I was as the doctor in that dynamic was never the question, but I have always wondered about the why. Why did a kid born into abject poverty and deprivation think he could become a heart surgeon? Why have I been so blessed yet plagued by a lingering sense of doubt? Yes, I can tell you how I accomplished certain things, but *why* looks behind the "apparel [that] was meant to be the curtain of the immortal soul," as Frost put it. How can any of us ever know for certain the why of things?

A sense of wonder is in itself a religious feeling. I've always felt a sense of wonder when the heart we were fixing started again. I have seen unexplainable turnarounds in the OR for dying patients. Is this in response to my prayers in that moment for the patient, or the 100% offering of skill and the sheer will of every dedicated professional in that room? Surely it was a Divine combination of all these factors. But what if that intervention didn't save the life? Why does it work sometimes but not others? Whatever answers a mortal man can find usually lead to more questions, at least for me they have.

Pascal said, "He who seeks God finds him." I guess I've spent my life exploring the different ways a statement like that could be understood. Poetry and literature have been my lexicons. I carry them in my briefcase. My collections are dog-eared. It's a rare day for me not to read from them. They're a refuge and it's probably not an overstatement to say the authors have been best friends of mine even if we never met in the flesh.

If I've kept my soul-searching to myself as much as possible, it's so my patients and family can come to me for answers—because they need me to be that man. Indeed, I have tried to be that man, and have been called to "carry the fire" all my life. But Wordsworth, Eliot, Emerson, Dostoevsky, Millay don't require that of me, and from them I learn not just "the wisdom of old men, but rather of their folly."

There is a kinship of doubt that makes good company along the way for one who is always searching for the answers he doesn't have. I am also that man. Now that I am looking back over eight decades of the journey, any remaining doubt is removing my "apparel" and having its way with me. Well, Eliot says, "The end is where we start from," so let that be how my story begins.

We shall not cease from exploration

And the end of all our exploring

Will be to arrive where we started

And know the place for the first time.

~ T.S. Eliot

As a child, Bill Reed baled hay and hoed beans in the fields around Kokomo. This is Mary Reed's grandparents' farming operation in rural Illinois, circa 1920.

CHAPTER 1

Beginnings

Man is but a reed,

the most feeble thing in nature,

but he is a thinking reed.

~ Pascal

The first poets I admired were the trees. It was a blessing to be surrounded by nature during childhood. It gave me a sensory vocabulary for things that couldn't be contained in words, by which I suppose I mean feelings, but even more than feelings. Does that make sense? For me, nature expresses truth in a way that explains joy, suffering, irony, and people. Growing up as I did, I had to work hard at understanding the world, and my place in it. I was born William Allen Reed on July 18, 1927, on the backside of Kokomo, Indiana, to a family too poor to feed another child. It was the summer of Babe Ruth, Charles Lindbergh, and Al Capone . . . just before the world went dark into the Depression.

We were already living in dire conditions before the Crash of 1929, but things went from bad to worse then. It was a hard-scrabble existence. There were eight of us kids, four to a bed inside the thin walls of the small frame sharecropper's cottage we rented. We had a coal-burning stove in the middle of the living room as the sole source of heat, and an unheated outhouse out back. There was never enough food and what we did have was often courtesy of local county assistance program. There were no special treats, birthday cakes, or Christmas presents, except for what came from the county. Once I got a light blue sweater, generically given to a "Boy, age 9," but I can't recall anything else except the raw feeling of not having what other families seemed to have. It was a stark, meager life made tolerable by my mother and a growing awareness of the beauty that I easily could have missed.

My mother Aldine helped me glimpse the bigger picture. She would show something beautiful just to me, of all her children. She would point out a rose or honeysuckle and in that pointing was a woman seeing more than her bitter, angry, unemployed husband and her hungry, anxious children. It was a vision she shared with me, a quiet leaf of a boy who desperately needed to see that there was more to life. That's what comes of reading trees and flowers and nature—a grasp of the finer side of one's circumstances and people. People are a lot like plants. Life has given me ample opportunity to gain fluency in this perspective.

There in the quiet hunger of my childhood, I was a detached observer of the passing scenes. I was raggedy, barefoot, underfed, and hollow-eyed with hair like oat straw. I felt estranged from much of life, a survival tactic no doubt. I cannot explain how I changed from that skinny, confused kid to the young man who decided he was going to be a doctor; or how I went from a doctor to one of the earliest successful heart surgeons, and then from the surgeon to a horseman raising racing thoroughbreds, and a philanthropist. A lot of people have asked me to tell the story of how I did that. If it helps anyone to read it, then it's worth a try.

Perhaps there were little signs early on; I would try to do more push-ups than anyone else and strive to get the highest grades. Of course, a lot of kids could make that claim, but in the end, I actually was one of those kids who did more push-ups and made the highest grades, even though no one really noticed. It did not come easy to me, in fact, it was very hard work. I was a scrawny, malnourished kid from the wrong side of the tracks. I don't recall anyone cheering me on from the sidelines. I wasn't invited to birthday parties and didn't excel in sports. Still I always wanted to be the best even if no one expected it from a kid of my station. Certainly, whatever I accomplished went unmarked by my father whose favorite saying about us kids—Lowell, Jimmy, Richard, William (or Bill, that's me), Jay, Mary, Wanda Sue, and Ervin—was that we were "useless as teats on a boar." If I was doing it to get his attention and approval that would have been the definition of useless.

My father, James Franklin Reed, was born in 1900 to a big time farm family from rural Kokomo. My grandfather shipped cattle to Kansas City in the early 1920s up until the Depression. Then they lost the farm and everything with it. Dad never recovered. He couldn't find or keep a regular job and roamed the countryside trying to make a go of dealing cattle.

It's hard to find anything really positive to say, but there's probably no way to avoid addressing certain realities about my emotionally-abusive father. The effort is "a raid on the inarticulate," as Eliot put it. Dad never had much of anything to say, but he was still intimidating—a big man, over six foot. I remember him in overalls weighing in at 275 pounds with a large abdomen, although I'm told he was quite an athlete in high school. He had a head of black hair that he parted on the side and combed straight back in the style of the day. I imagine my mother found him charming at first. Something of that charm was what he used later in life to finagle farmers out of their cattle. And he did know cattle—well enough to guess the weight of a steer right down to the pound while he wheeled and dealed some guy out of the prize of his herd.

I try to be compassionate, to imagine what it felt like to have no way of providing for eight children and a wife. Some say it drove him to drink. I know it made him angry, and he focused his anger at the world on his family. My dad could get mad at you over ten bucks you owed him and not talk to you for a year. Folks avoided him, even his own siblings and parents. Even after we'd all grown up and gone, my brothers, sisters and I would come back to visit at the holidays and no one would talk to him, not a word. My dad would just sit in a rocking chair at their old house waiting until we were gone . . . just sit there staring angrily at a world he thought owed him something.

As far as I know, I was the only kid in the family who really related to my dad in a day to day sense because I'd help him with the cows. Being from a cattle family, he loved cows. Depending on where we were living, sometimes we'd have a few. I was the one he had pump the water by hand for them, feed them, and help with milking. Through that connection, you'd think I might have known my father a little more, but we never had any meaningful discussion about anything. I was too scared of him, and he wasn't interested anyway. I can't remember a happy time with him, not a single conversation that lasted more than a few minutes, and never anything remotely paternal or philosophical.

My mother worked hard at making up for what her husband lacked. She was born Aldine Caroline Little in 1899 to a poor farming family in rural Indiana. She was quiet and small, just five feet tall and 100 pounds. She was bright although she attended school only through the eighth grade. Mother never wore a stitch of make-up and always had an apron on over a faded print dress. She devoted her life to her children, even though she didn't have the luxury of spending a lot of time with us. Without much help from Dad, pulling the weight was more than a full time job. Her sister would help out sometimes.

My aunt was over one winter night when my little brother Jimmy and I both had whooping cough so bad we couldn't breathe. She took me outside in the cold air to cut the cough. Somehow I survived. Not every child did, and that's how we lost Jimmy. He was just over four years old when he died.

Mother was usually the only one who brought in any money; she worked herself to the bone as a restaurant cook. In every kind of weather, she walked two and a half miles each way to work. As hard as she worked, it was only once a week that we could afford to have some kind of meat with our dinner. I can recall standing by my mother once as she cooked some sausage and telling her how great it was we could have that meal. She started crying. It made me feel so bad because I was really just trying to make her feel good.

My love and respect for my mother were deep, and the feeling was mutual. We had a similar mentality and a sense of Thoreau's "quiet desperation" in common. On one occasion, prompted by something I can't even recall, we were sharing how terrible life would be if the other of us died first. She was as distraught by the idea of that as I was. Perhaps she felt the same way about my siblings, but she had a way of making me feel special and I cherished this. She was a rock in my foundation, and I feared losing her . . . probably because there was never any sense of security with my dad. To his credit, he never left us. During the Depression, many men did abandon their families. At least Dad stuck around.

Mother used to tell us that Dad walked the streets everyday looking for a job. That was probably an embellishment—her attempt to keep us from being so disappointed in him. She did her best to protect us from him. I'd wake up in the early hours of morning and they'd be arguing about things. He'd be yelling, screaming and stomping around the house, and there was my tiny mother trying to hold her ground. They were always fighting about us kids . . . what we needed. We came first for her, and she fought for us. But that was an era when the man wore the pants in the family, and he was a tyrant. I don't recall that he ever struck her, but the emotional cruelty was hard enough. Once he was upset with my brother Rick about something and hit him with a buggy whip. It left a deep twelve inch gash across his shoulders. Dad was downright mean, and he'd make me so upset that at one point I told my mother I'd had all I could take and was getting out of there. She knew I didn't have any place to go, but she'd beg me not to go anyway. All of us felt that way more than once. We wanted out of there desperately but Mom would beg us not to go. Out of loyalty to her, we stayed until some form of escape was justified.

A child of poverty does not dream of excess, only of enough. In fact, the only dream I can remember having was about getting a meal. That required money, so even as a little boy I worked at whatever job could be had. In the summer, I'd hoe weeds out of soy beans for five cents an hour. If my brothers and I could scrape some extra money together, we would buy a can of pineapple because it was Mom's favorite thing. We tried to make her happy, but we were normal boys into whatever mischief kids can get into, like hoisting some fellow's car onto the train tracks to cut across town or some such nonsense. It's a wonder we never got ourselves killed.

Somebody in the gang I ran with discovered that if you pressed hard on a vein in the neck, you could make a guy pass out. We didn't know why it would happen, but of course it was due to closing off the blood supply to the brain. I don't even know why we did it, except in a world without money for movies or bowling, that's the sort of thing that constituted entertainment—that and racing cars. No matter how poor or hungry you were, if you drove fast or hung with the guys who did, you enjoyed a certain status in the rabble of smalltime Hoosier life. It was a tentative position, and I can clearly recall a buddy of mine climbing over the seats to get behind the wheel and overtake a car that had passed us as we all barreled down some country road. Reputations were at stake, and he saved ours that night.

Maybe if she'd known how crazy we were, my mother would have tried to impose some limitations, but parents didn't hover over their kids back then like they do now. She would never tell us we couldn't do something, that wasn't her style. She'd just say, "You know you have to get up and go to work in the morning." The way she loved her children was as quiet and pensive as she was about everything else in her life. She worried, no doubt, but didn't express her feelings easily. The entire time I was growing up I can never remember my mother actually telling me she loved me, although I knew she did. My dad never said so either, and I thought he didn't.

Perhaps it's a generational thing, but love wasn't expressed between parents and children in those days like it is today. When my mother's father died, we all went to the funeral. My mother looked at me after the service and said, "You didn't even cry!" Well, how can a seven year old understand what death is about? I'd only seen my grandfather three times in my life, how was I supposed to feel? Was death supposed to prompt feelings I didn't even know I had? Was crying from emotion or obligation? What happened to grandpa after he died? If he went to heaven, why was my mother so upset? I just looked at the floor feeling confused and detached from what was clearly a major life event, unable to comprehend it. My mind tried to work out what it all meant but couldn't. Then life just went on.

At one point, we were so poor we had to move into a church basement in Kokomo. It was during the Depression, and we had no other place to live. We were on county assistance for food, but there was no allowance for rent, so this was the best we could do. The arrangement must have put some pressure on my mother to attend the church, but I don't recall that we ever did. We weren't a church-going family, although we did rely on its charity as well as government assistance. We tried to joke about it . . . whose turn it was to wear the socks . . . or how mother would always ask for "two bags, please" when the garbage man came by.

I don't remember how long we lived in that basement before we moved again. There was a lot of moving around, it goes that way with those who can't afford to make the rent. One of the places we lived brought a substantial improvement to my life: I finally made a best friend.

His name was Junior Ross, but I called him Nip. He called me Knucklehead. I didn't think of him as a poor black kid, even though he was, and he didn't think of me as a rich, privileged white kid because I definitely wasn't. At that time, my family lived on the wrong side of town in a scrubby bungalow across the alley from Nip's family who were as destitute as we were. I'd go over to his house and there in the front room was the daybed where his brother D'Boy was dying from tuberculosis. Out back was a dilapidated trailer where some new "daddy" would live until Nip's mom kicked him out.

Not sure how my dad managed this, but for a while he had a sorrel pony named Ted with a little cart. My brothers and I would lead kids around the city park for five cents a ride. Nip would always come with us until my older brother said he didn't want Nip tagging along because people were talking—the park was segregated and blacks weren't allowed. I was too young to question why—I'm not sure I even noticed such things. So instead, Nip and I switched to looking for junk in the alleyways to sell and make enough money for both of us to go to the movies. We had to sit in different places until the lights went off then I'd move back to where he was. That there was a section delegated for blacks didn't prompt any deep philosophical thoughts on injustice within me . . . the Civil Rights Movement would come later. I was incredibly naïve about such things. I just wanted to be with my buddy, and that's where I had to sit in order to be with Nip.

In retrospect, it was unusual to be raised without racial prejudice during that era, and I can't say that my folks deserve any credit for that. The truth is, they were oblivious to my goings on and never weighed in on the subject. Their focus on basic survival wasn't conducive to monitoring my movements and friendships very closely. I certainly don't remember being admonished to stay away from black people. As a result, I didn't, so I was free to experience my first real friendship with a boy whose skin was a different color than mine. Nip was always laughing and fun-loving. He never had a chip on his shoulder about his circumstances. It was just easy being around a kid like that. It imprinted a very positive message in my mind about the importance of one's outlook. All of my life, I have been blessed by a profound sense of "colorblindness" that I credit to my first best friend Nip who taught me to see the person, not a skin color.

Some of the kids from my neighborhood—both black and white—ended up in prison. I owe a lot to Mr. Thompson, my machine shop teacher, for showing me a different path. In those days, if you didn't have any plans to go to college you took industrial courses in school. High school graduation wasn't a given for kids like me, much less going onto college, so I was on the vocational track—no math, no language arts, no preparation for anything but the labor force.

Chet Thompson was a stocky, no nonsense fellow who was very serious about his teaching. I spent hours in his machine shop. I learned a lot about machining, but even more about myself. Mr. Thompson saw something promising in me and took the time to nurture it. Aside from my mother, he was the only adult during my youth who ever did. Every Thursday, he'd take me along to the Lion's Club for lunch. It was the only decent meal I had all week. He even took me to a football game at Purdue once. He managed to do all this without making me feel like a charity case; instead I felt something emerging that I didn't know was called "self-worth." It seeded a sense of purpose within me. This is what can happen when someone positively reflects your abilities back to you . . . you begin to see yourself as a capable person and then the possibilities grow.

A good education can and should imbue that in every student. When it does, education is certainly the most likely way out of poverty. You may find it in the formal sense in institutions, but also in the people you meet along the way. The instinct and inclination to learn are programmed into every human being, as I see it. Teachers who can effectively tap into that are the ones who combine their content knowledge with inspiration and validation of the student him or herself. Without that from Chet Thompson, there was no way I could have believed I was capable of more than my limitations. That might have been the most important lesson I learned in school.

> *What's nice about working for Dr. Reed is that he's self-made. Most people with money don't understand what life is like for those without it. He does. He gets it, and he respects me because I also came from a poor family and learned how to work hard.*
>
> *~ Garrett Smith, Stonecrest Farm Manager*

There are people who say school isn't for them, but the ones who really want to learn need help recognizing the door is open to them, at least I did. I was always more intent on escaping poverty than dwelling on it. One does not escape from poverty without help from loving, caring people. For me there was a special teacher, and eventually others helped by reaching out at different times of my life. That was a blessing because my parents weren't able to do that for me. Education was the key to my escape.

In high school, I got a job as paperboy for the *Indianapolis Star* and the *Kokomo Tribune*. We'd get so many pennies per paper, so I maximized my profits by employing a two wheel push cart instead of a bicycle. After filling it up at the distribution center, I'd take off on my route by 6:00 am. On Sundays, I timed my stop at the Catholic Church right before mass got out. In the winter, I could keep warm in the upstairs hallway until it was over. Even though my family didn't attend church, sometimes I'd go to that church by myself. I was never compelled to become a member, but it was a good place to sit and listen and ponder.

When your stomach is empty, as mine usually was, your hierarchy of need is food, not a grasp of the meaning of life. Still, the books I was drawn to in high school were the soul searching kind. Somerset Maugham's *The Razor's Edge*, a lot of Hemingway, T.S. Eliot, and Wordsworth all spoke to me. I related to Kafka's views on the absurdity of life and its trials that show us there is no hope to be found on earth, so we must look beyond our literal circumstances to find some kind of spiritual meaning. The search itself was unavoidable. My entre to poetry and philosophy was no doubt some early crush on a girl that never lasted. The poems and perspectives of the great writers did.

At some point, I got a hold of *Dr. Hudson's Secret Journal* and decided his philosophy also made sense. The point was that whatever good you did in the world only counted if you didn't make a spectacle of it. My father was the antithesis of that. He'd boast about taking advantage of some farmer or how much smarter he was than everybody else. No doubt his own insecurities were at the root of this, but his braggadocio was excruciating for me. It was just one more trait I hoped I didn't inherit.

By example, my mother modeled a simple love and an appreciation of beauty. By contrast, my father also profoundly influenced the way I would experience the world. Ironically, his meanness and self-regard taught me a lot about the critical importance of compassion, generosity and love. Maybe he deserves as much credit as my mother for providing the motivation to go in search of life's meaning. I knew I had to do something to break out of that mold.

If you wish to advance

into the infinite

explore the finite

in all directions

~ Goethe

It was hard to reconcile the bleak reality of my childhood with my profound sense of beauty, wonder and aspiration for a life beyond my circumstances; but it was the spring of 1945, and those circumstances were about to change.

I think with Bill and my husband Jay, their dad became the example of how they didn't want to live. Given their difficult childhood, they all wanted more. They were all hard workers, every one of them, and they were going to be different from their father.

~ Lucy Reed, sister-in-law

Grandma Reed was proud of him . . . and he had a special fondness for his mother. But it was strained with his dad who was kind of an ass. We'd go visit them and he'd order my dad out into the field to help him corral an old bull, so there was my dad the surgeon running around a big field doing what his dad asked him to do. My grandfather never was impressed by my dad's accomplishments. He never demonstrated any love for his son at all. It was remarkable to me because my father was such an amazing dad with us.

~ Jeff Reed, oldest son

My dad said he was going to break the cycle of his alcoholic father. There was something inside him and my Uncle Bill that was probably related to their faith.

~ Greg Reed, nephew

Bill Reed in 1945

Campus Studio, Bloomington, Indiana

CHAPTER 2

Young Man

When you grow up like Bill and I did,
you want to get out of that.

~ *William "Bill" Hamaker, MD*
Heart Surgeon (retired), St. Luke's Hospital

I did manage to graduate from Kokomo High School in May of 1945 just in time to enlist for the end of World War II. Two of my brothers were in the Air Force, but I joined the Navy just to try something different. I was in boot camp in Chicago when the atomic bombs were dropped on Hiroshima and Nagasaki. Those were frightening times–the future was here, and it was unimaginable. I was given aptitude tests and directed to sign on as a motor machinist mate. It took me two and a half days on a train from Chicago to Seattle to report for duty. That was the first I'd seen of the world outside Indiana. I'm not sure I ever shut my eyes the whole trip, and there at the end of it was the ocean and the ship that would be my next home.

My battle station was five levels down in the engine room of the USS Nevada, a huge battleship that would later be used in further atomic testing at the Bikini Atoll. There were guys ratcheting down the water-tight doors four levels above . . . it was a bad place to be if you were claustrophobic. Fortunately for me they were a good group of guys. There'd always be one of them in the resupply group pitching some extra grub down the gangway so we had more to eat. I never once complained about military food. When I entered the Navy, I weighed 120 pounds soaking wet, but after a year of three meals a day, I was 185 in my skivvies. Eating regularly remade my physique, and there was another big change . . . I got baptized.

There was a space on the ship for Christian services, although it didn't look like a church. It was just an area used for that. One of the guys on the "black gang"—as those of us working in the engine room were called—had a minister's license and he was constantly evangelizing. This was my first real experience with anything like that. I hoped it would bring answers to some of the deeper questions brewing within me. Before I knew it, another fellow and I found ourselves converted to the Baptist faith. It wasn't a spiritual experience for me . . . more of an "empty prayers" kind of ritual that I hoped might lead to some sort of enlightenment. I really don't recall why I did it considering I didn't have a religious feeling about it. I wanted to find some answers to my search for meaning, so it seemed the thing to do.

Back home, my high school girlfriend Beverly anxiously awaited my first leave . . . perhaps a little too anxiously. She was my first love, and we had been writing each other ever since I left for the service. I was an old-fashioned guy and would never push the advantage of our long absence, although I sensed Beverly wished that I would. I just wasn't ready for that level of commitment, so we parted ways. I never really lacked for feminine attention during those years, but there was no doubt in my mind how far a guy could take things before he had crossed into the zone of obligation. I wasn't going there until I was ready to make that kind of commitment to the right kind of girl. I didn't know what my own course would be, much less how to manage things as a couple.

By August of 1946, my enlistment was up. I struggled with what I would do when I got out of the Navy. I just couldn't envision a life back in Kokomo fixing engines, but I didn't know what else to do. There were the spit-and-polish fellas with lots of medals giving all of us guys the "shipping-over-music" about how great the Navy was so we would re-enlist for active duty. And there was factory back home, which seemed a likely possibility. The night before I was discharged, I lay in my berth staring at the rivets of the steel walls and feeling like I'd been breathing the same air in that compartment for twelve months. I was busting to get out, but I didn't have a clue what would happen to me next. I figured I'd have to stay on with the Navy Reserve, what other choice was there?

Lying there on the top bunk, the limitations of possibility seemed as low as the grey ceiling a foot from my face. If joining thoughts of helplessness with hopefulness is a kind of prayer, then I was praying with all my might. In what I would later come to recognize as Divine guidance, I heard a voice. It spoke audibly, but only to me. It might have been my own voice, but it wasn't familiar to me in the literal sense. The voice was saying I wanted to be a doctor. It was a brand new idea, and I had no idea where it came from, but there it was.

I wanted to be a doctor.

It never occurred to me that I could actually set a goal that high for myself. I never dreamed of going to college much less medical school. Up until that moment, I'd never had a single thought about going into medicine. What prompted me to think of this? The only thing I can say is that I have come to believe that many people have a sense of calling to do the work they do, and sometimes they even experience "a call" to service—this is not a thing that happens only to those in ministry. While I never considered being a doctor before that night, the feeling that came to me was powerful and certain. Oddly, it never occurred to me to think I couldn't do it. Not only did I feel that I could—although God only knows where that confidence came from—but I had a strong sense that I should—that I was supposed to be a doctor. There's just no explanation for this except that I had responded to a sense of calling.

Being a heart surgeon was what I was destined to do. I know that sounds more religious and assured than I purport to be, but I've seen enough evidence to back the claim even if I struggle to articulate how this all works. I think the human spirit is something that has no limitations even if one's circumstances suggest otherwise. The odds of my being a heart surgeon would have been one in ten million . . . unbelievably small. Yet that's exactly what happened. Yes, I worked hard as is my nature, but without the voice of something bigger and stronger than me—a higher power directing me—I wouldn't have applied that ability to medicine.

I made my plan. After I got out of the Navy, I knew I'd be eligible for two years of college funding thanks to the GI Bill, but it would take four years to get a degree. I didn't have any other money. So I did start working at American Standard as a plumbing parts inspector, and I picked up another part-time job at the steel mill a mile away. For two years I lived at home working and saving money. I took classes at the Indiana University Extension Center to fill in the gaps from courses I didn't get in high school, and to complete courses that would be required for entrance to medical school. I bought a used algebra book and taught myself the math I'd need to pass the college-level courses at Indiana University where I transferred for my junior and senior years.

If you had your required courses, you could apply for medical school after three years, which I did but I wasn't accepted. So I had to finish my fourth year and try again. I have often reflected on this when talking to people who tell me they weren't accepted into medical school . . . did they try again? I didn't get in until my second attempt after I graduated in 1950 with a degree in Chemistry. How different my life would have been if I'd given up on the first try.

All of the Reed kids were successful—a nurse, a licensed dental technician, an advertising executive, a tool and die maker, a clothing store owner, and a service manager—which is a credit to their mother. She was so proud of all of them.

~ Lucy Reed, sister-in-law

In the fall of 1950, I started medical school at Indiana University in Bloomington. I carried about twenty-two hours each semester for the first two years, which was a heavy load. One of the guys I shared living quarters with was the sort who would load up the back end of his truck with a mattress and beer and he'd take off with some girl for the weekend. He would show up late Sunday night and ask what we had to know for the test on Monday—the very one I'd been studying for all weekend. I'd say head and neck, or some such thing. He'd say ok, then just waltz in and ace it. I sure envied him.

During my freshman year of med school, the Korean War broke out. I was still enlisted in the Navy Reserve as a motor machinist mate, and got a call back to active duty. In order to get a deferment and stay in med school, I had to accept a position as Lieutenant Junior Grade in the Navy Reserve. The war in Korea ended in 1953 just as I was finishing the last year of med school so I didn't get called back to active duty.

Med school was pretty intense, so sometimes Dad and the other interns would blow off steam with pranks, like the time they rigged up a string to the penis of a cadaver to shock a female med student. She ran out of the room! He doesn't like me to tell that story on him, but it was true.

~ Jeff Reed

When I was in my second year, I had rented a room with a widow and her family. I took meals with them and stayed there a full semester before I got a job at Norways Sanitarium, a private psychiatric hospital which was operated out of an old mansion on the east side of Indianapolis. This was when the theory of medicine really started becoming the practice because I was seeing patients in clinics with the attending physicians at Indiana University Medical Center.

As medical students, we wore the traditional "whites" and went on-call with a small medicine bag. I had my first stethoscope and was starting to feel like a real doctor. I especially liked delivering babies. On one of those calls, the seasoned mother well into her labor informed me, "Son, if you'll just get out of my way, I'm going to have this baby." And she did. Women have been delivering babies without doctors as long as there have been babies, a fact I've always kept in mind. Still, there were cases where it could have gone badly without some help, as with a homeless woman in a little shanty in an alley of downtown Indianapolis. People were walking along the sidewalk six or eight feet away and I was trying to get that baby out. There was no decent surface area, nothing remotely sanitized, and all I had to put under the mom was a newspaper. Some improvisation could be necessary, and that was something of a specialty for me. She was successfully delivered of a strong baby boy.

It was the time of the polio epidemic, and I got a part-time job doing special duty nursing that involved caring for patients inside the iron lungs. Essentially, I was the muscle and the nurses were the brains. I moved from my lodgings with the widow's family over to the fourth floor of the Norways. I was thinking that I'd focus on psychiatry because it seemed to be such an interesting specialization. To cover the costs of my room and board, I drew blood on patients in the early morning, then I went on to classes at medical school. On Saturdays, I picked up extra work for spending money at Methodist Hospital doing electro-encephalograms—brain tracings on the patients. Of course, all work and no play make Jack a dull boy, so I'd go out with some of the student nurses I met as they'd go through a psychiatric rotation, but I never got serious with any of them until Mary Shear.

Before he met Mom, Dad squired around the nurses. His standard pick up line was, "Kiss me, baby, nothing makes me sick."

~ Jeff Reed

It was the spring of 1952, I was playing ping pong with a patient in the rehab room at Norways when a nurse I hadn't seen before walked through the room. Her name was Mary Shear and she was gorgeous in her crisp white uniform, the starched nurse's cap crowning her dark hair. I just stood there gaping as the ball went whizzing by.

My memories of Mary often begin with what she was wearing. I might not even recall where we were—some social event that doctors and their wives had to be seen at—but I can still tell you how the heads would turn to see this stunning woman on my arm in a saffron lace gown. Whatever it was, a yellow dress or her nurse's whites, Mary's beauty and presence made it remarkable. She was as striking as a movie star, a brunette with smiling brown eyes, ivory skin—along the lines of Elizabeth Taylor, but more wholesome like Donna Reed. Anyone who has ever known her would tell you Mary is even more beautiful on the inside. From the moment I met her, all the girls I'd been squiring around just ceased to matter to me. I still had medical school to finish, but began formulating a plan for what I'd do afterwards. Mary Shear would factor heavily into that.

Mary Shear in 1955

CHAPTER 3

The Right Girl

"None of this was possible without Mary.
How did Hemingway put it,
'Thou art all there will be of me'?"

~ *William Reed*

When I first saw Bill, he was playing ping pong at Norways
Sanitarium where I was a student nurse. He had an odd-look
on his face, not quite a smile. To tell the truth, I thought he was
one of the patients. It was definitely not love at first sight, but
that is how I met the love of my life.

~ *Mary Shear Reed, wife*

In many ways, Mary Shear was born to be a doctor's wife. Intelligent, beautiful, socially graceful, and a skilled registered nurse, she could relate to my work. She was also a devoted mother content to raise the children and keep the home fires burning while I put in long hours at the hospital. Growing up as the daughter of a rigidly demanding, emotionally-unavailable father, Mary learned early to be a pleaser. The upside of that was a selfless, compassionate nature that would become her hallmark.

She was born Mary Josephine on October 31, 1930, in the rural farming town of Thawville, Illinois, the oldest of two daughters born to Asay and Pauline Shear. Her younger sister Mardell came along seven years later.

Her mother Pauline Martin had just graduated from high school when she married Asay Shear, the son of Swiss immigrants. He was a sophomore in college at the time. Eventually, he earned a Master's degree and became a schoolteacher. Asay had strong values for education and constantly made Pauline feel inferior for her lack of higher education. With his daughter Mary, he was a strict, critical father. Asay had a tendency to get livid over anything . . . everyone tip-toed around him to keep from setting him off. Mary worked hard at being perfect to meet his expectations.

Everything Mary did was in hopes of pleasing her father and gaining his approval, which he never gave. Lacking this from him, she basked in the warmth and acceptance she found at church. Her Bible school teacher finally called Pauline to ask when Mary's birthday was since every week her little hand went up when it was time to sing to the children who were celebrating birthdays.

However detached her father was, Asay's parents were entirely devoted to their granddaughter and provided the loving environment she craved. Her grandmother was from Switzerland, and while she had been very strict with her sons, she was lovingly nurturing with Mary. Her granddad was a builder with a crew that did construction of homes, farms, and even a theatre in a nearby town. Mary's happiest summers were those spent in Thawville with Grandpa and Grandma Shear. She developed her lovely singing voice while doing dishes with her grandmother. Mary felt her grandparents loved her unconditionally. Time with them was a wonderful respite from the austerity of the atmosphere back home with her parents and sister.

Whereas Asay was strict and demanding of Mary, he was indulgent with her little sister. Mardell was adorable with blonde curls compared to Mary's serious brown eyes and straight, dark hair. He would berate Mary for one A-minus on a report card otherwise full of A-plus grades while accepting Mardell's B's and C's without issue.

A defining moment in Mary's young life happened one Sunday over dinner. The whole family was gathered around the table, even her beloved grandparents were there. Mary said something grammatically incorrect. Asay announced in front of the whole group that even Mardell wouldn't have made such a mistake. The embarrassment and shame Mary felt was made even worse because not one person stood up for her. Not even her grandmother dared speak out against Asay. Mary ran out of the house and far into a field where she fell crying into the grass.

Even now it makes me cry to think about that day. I felt like nobody loved me, not even my grandmother. But as I sat there in the grass, I realized that Jesus loved me. And I had a Heavenly Father who loved me, so it didn't matter if anybody else did or not. I remember thinking it was actually wonderful that this happened because that's how I knew God loved me and it didn't matter if nobody else did. That was the exact moment when I turned myself over and knew I was God's child. My faith has never wavered. I have always known it since that day.

~ Mary Reed

After that epiphany, Mary would regularly go out to a bluff near her home and spend time talking to God. She always said it was where she felt most at peace.

The Shears moved to Wayne, Michigan, when Mary was in high school. Pauline went back to school to become a cosmetologist.

Every day after school, Mary had to watch her younger sister, get dinner going, and finish her homework. She managed, but was still never able to impress her Father. He did enjoy it when Mary sang and even liked to harmonize with her. Those were Mary's best memories of her dad . . . when she sang solos at church and he seemed proud of her.

Pauline was completely oppressed by her husband, but she encouraged her daughter as best she could. For Mary's first prom, her mother had presented her with a black velvet coat with gold sequins to go with Mary's black and white checkered dress. It was a rare thing for Mary to be the sole focus of such attention—that was usually Mardell's spot.

Mardell and Mary were never close, partly due to the age difference, but Mardell was spoiled and she had a mean streak that always strained the relationship. She once crushed Mary's treasured radio—a gift from her grandparents—and kicked her foot through the window when Mary didn't do her bidding. Even though Mary was sick in bed at the time, when Pauline got home from work and saw the cuts on Mardell's leg, Mary was the one who got in trouble. The dynamics between the girls, and their parents' favoritism of Mardell, reinforced Mary's insecurity. It made her try even harder to please her mom and dad.

In Asay Shear's family, it was expected that you'd go to college. He wanted Mary to be a doctor. In Mary's only act of rebellion, she insisted that she wanted to be a nurse. And so she did, but instead of celebrating her achievement, Asay saw only a compromise. Given her penchant for wanting to please him, I think it's remarkable that she held her ground on this one.

> *I can't recall ever once earning respect or approval from my dad, or his love. He never expressed those feelings verbally, even though I believe he did love me in his own way. I felt that I had to work hard to be loved and even with my best effort, I never seemed to be good enough for my father.*
>
> *~ Mary Reed*

Mary went to nursing school at Ball State University. During her last three years, she worked full time at Ball Memorial Hospital in Muncie. She wasn't poor, but she had no money for anything extra. She told me she wore the same clothes for four years with one exception: her mother sent her a package with yellow pedal pushers and a green formal dress. The pedal pushers were darling, Mary recalled, and the formal was for her to wear as a contestant for Ball State's Blue Key Sweetheart. Mary wasn't a sorority girl, and it was unusual for a nursing student to be chosen as a candidate for this BSU honor. She didn't win, but the real treasure was the acknowledgment and support from her mom. I wish we had a picture of her in that pageant, but we don't.

Being a doctor's wife . . . it came very naturally for me.

~ Mary Reed

*M*ary would be the first to tell you I was very quiet and not comfortable socially with a lot of people. Whereas she had been involved in everything in high school, I wasn't. Mary was popular, busy, accepted by good students and into every club. She was in graduate nursing school and already engaged to somebody else when we met. But the relationship was fizzling out and she gave that guy's ring back.

As Mary recalls it, I was nice looking and pleasant so she went out with me. I had dated plenty of the other nurses, but Mary was special. She was the right kind of girl. After our first date, I put my hands gently on each side of her face and kissed her goodnight. Now Mary wasn't the kind of girl who let a guy kiss her on the first date, but somehow she apparently felt it might just be ok to kiss me . . . and after I kissed her, she was certain of it. That's the way she tells the story. I still smile to think of it.

We dated about two years, and although we talked about getting married, I never actually proposed. This issue became a source of tension between us. At one point, Mary called her grandmother in frustration asking if she could come for the weekend—she needed time away from me. Grandma Shear told her to get on a bus and she'd pay for the tickets. Grandpa and Grandma Shear were always there for her. After a couple days cocooned in their safe haven at Thawville, Mary returned to Indianapolis where she focused on her nursing job in obstetrics and gynecology at Coleman Hospital at Indiana University Medical Center. I had to charm my way back into her good graces. She can be tough; you'd be surprised how tough Mary can be at times.

I knew I had the right girl, but I didn't want to get married until I had completed medical school. I felt that it wouldn't be fair to Mary, so I didn't press the issue. The Christmas before my graduation, Mary still didn't see our relationship going anywhere and started making other plans. She told me she was going home to her parents in Michigan to get a job. That's precisely when I handed her a ring and said matter of factly, "Take this with you and set the date." I wish I'd been more romantic, and I'm pretty sure Mary does, too.

> *God has a plan for all of us, but he gives us the freedom to choose which way we go. I prayed a lot before I married Bill to make sure he was the right person to marry.*
>
> *~ Mary Reed*

On April 4, 1954, we were married in the Indianapolis Methodist Church, right after my graduation. Mary was almost twenty-four, and I was twenty-six. We drove to Bloomington for a one-night honeymoon because I had to be back to work the next day. When the weekend came around, Mary ended up having her wisdom teeth removed. I went fishing with a buddy. Mary says, "It wasn't a very romantic start to wedded life, but that's just how it happened!" When we speak of it over sixty years later, we both smile.

> *They were an attractive couple. He was the young resident and she was a skilled nurse. They were the Samson and Delilah of the medical center.*
>
> *~ Gunner Proud, MD*
> *Former Chairman, Ear, Nose and Throat Department, KUMC*

> *It's kind of a fairy tale . . . KU resident doctor marries the prettiest nurse.*
>
> *~ Bill Hamaker, MD*
> *Heart Surgeon and Reed's former medical partner*

We lived for the first few months in a small duplex in Indianapolis. I finished medical school three months early and worked at the state mental hospital. Psychiatry appealed to me, and I thought my career would head in that direction. Mary was working as a nurse at the Veterans Administration Hospital. I had been thinking about doing a psychiatric residency at Menninger's Psychiatric Institute in Topeka, so in July 1954, I accepted an internship at the University of Kansas (KU) Hospital. In true D.H. Lawrence fashion, we headed west. Mary also got work at KU as an instructor for OB-GYN nursing students and she became the main breadwinner.

> *Bill's mother never accepted me. Just before we got married, the girls gave me a shower. She came and announced out of the blue, "I don't think Bill's going to go through with this." It was awkward and I was devastated. I guess she wanted somebody close to home. I tried to develop a relationship with her, but it never came to anything. Bill's theory was that as his wife I reaped all the benefits of his success. After all the struggle of her own life, she felt entitled to more of the rewards.*
>
> *~ Mary Reed*

*M*ary and I wanted to have a family of our own and finally felt settled enough in our careers to try. But we were not successful. As our professional achievements increased, the personal sense of failure over not having a child was one Mary felt most keenly. My sadness was real, but year after year without a baby was unbearably painful for my wife.

> *When I lost our first baby, I was angry with myself . . . how could my body reject a child? I remember praying, God, you know how bad I want a child, why did this happen? I lost the baby at five and a half months. It didn't seem to bother Bill as much, or else he was handling it better than me, but I was devastated.*
>
> ~ *Mary Reed*

As an obstetrics nurse, Mary had access to the best resources on fertility and her medical colleagues recommended all kinds of things to help her conceive. Five years later, nothing had worked. At that point, Mary and I were in our thirties and we were giving up. In those days, it was considered unsafe to be an older mother, a *primigravada*, for both mother and child. The OB-GYN doctor she worked for suggested adoption. We discussed it, got comfortable with the idea, and filled out the paperwork. Both of us felt a growing excitement that we might finally become parents. Before long, we got a call.

> *The adoption agency wanted to know if we would consider a baby who was part Native American. We didn't even hesitate. We saw Jeff and he was so cute, those long eye lashes. He was my baby. I didn't even know I was pregnant when we brought him home. I lost that baby at three months, but I had Jeff. He was the happiest baby. Bill would come home late and wake him up to play. Jeff would be so happy any time of the day or night.*
>
> ~ *Mary Reed*

Born on May 21, 1961, Jeffrey Howard became a Reed when he was six weeks old. Mary gave him her father's middle name as his own. We just felt instantly that he was our baby. Jeff's biological parents had been college students. His birth mother was of Native American heritage. We never kept the adoption a secret from Jeff, but there was a point during his childhood when his birth history needed to be shared. Mary found the teachable moment when Jeff was about eight. Ginger, his German Shepherd puppy, got hit on the road and Jeff was completely distraught. Mary prayed for words, and realized she could share how she came to understand her own infertility issues. She sat Jeff down and explained there must be another puppy he was supposed to have . . . how hurt she had been when she lost her own baby, but there was another baby God wanted them to have and that was Jeff. He understood.

> *Although I was adopted and I didn't resemble my dad physically, I always felt I was the child of his heart. He was both father and mother to me when my mom was confined to bed while she was pregnant with Bryan. He has always been there for me, right from the start.*
>
> *~ Jeff Reed*

Jeff was nearly a year old when Mary got pregnant again. Given her risk-factors, she was put on strict bed-rest in order to carry the baby to full term. I took over Jeff-duty, which was not standard-operating-procedure in that era. I was cool as a cucumber at the hospital, but had the same worries any parent would have when it came to problems with my own child. I'll never forget the time he swallowed something that got stuck in his throat and obstructed his breathing. He was choking and turning blue, so I had to reach in with my fingers to pull it out. It's a very different thing to do that to your own child than to a patient in the ER. The last thing I wanted was for Mary to have to worry about him, so I down-played anything that could make her anxious. That was the year we had Christmas up in the bedroom.

When Bryan was born, I thought 'I have finally done something perfect.'

~ Mary Reed

Bryan Allen Reed was born on February 5, 1963, in Kansas City, Kansas. He was followed by our third son, William Martin Reed, on August 19, 1964. With two babies in diapers plus a three year old to chase down, Mary's agenda necessarily changed. Her mother came briefly after each baby was born to help out, although I'm not sure Pauline's presence wasn't just added pressure. At one point, one of the babies was working up a good cry after he'd been laid into the crib at bedtime. I urged Mary to just let him settle himself for a minute or two. I don't think Mary's restraint lasted even a minute before Pauline sounded the alarm: Are you going to let that baby cry all night?

In truth, Mary managed very well without her mother's help. She was a natural at mothering. Jeff-duty aside, it was more of a challenge for me. I was good at helping when the boys got bigger, giving them their baths, helping with homework, and putting them to bed.

When my boys were tiny, they were all mine. Bill was better with them after they got a bit older and started talking. But when they were babies, they were just all mine.

~ Mary Reed

Eager to please as the doctor's ideal wife, Mary had maintained perfect hair, makeup, meals, and clothes—both mine and hers—for the first seven years of our marriage. Although the priorities shifted now that we had three little ones, somehow Mary kept the house warm and inviting—ready to entertain hospital VIPs or other guests at a moment's notice. I suspect there was a fair amount of stress involved that she kept from me. Mary made extraordinary efforts to be a perfect hostess, so when my mother came to visit and commented, "Oh, it's easy enough to do if you've got money," Mary was understandably hurt. I think my mother was envious, if not jealous; it made things awkward at times.

A lot of other doctors I knew would hang around the hospital even if they didn't need to be there. I would do my job then come home. Family was my priority. It was rare to sit down to dinner without me at the table. As a nurse herself, Mary understood the demands on my schedule. She never nagged me about missing something on the homefront because I had to be at the hospital. She understood, and the children did, too, that if I wasn't home it was because someone needed me badly.

> *I loved to hear him share everything that was happening at work so I could experience it, too. I never ever expected him to get up with the kids. I had his breakfast ready so he could go in rested and strong for his work. I wanted to be a part of his life that way. I wanted things smooth here at home so he could devote all his energy to his work.*
>
> *~ Mary Reed*

Bryan, Martin and Jeff Reed, Edinburgh, 1967

CHAPTER 4

Family Man

The world stands out on either side

no wider than the heart is wide

~ *Edna St. Vincent Millay*

I didn't want to be like my father; nor did I want to be Dr. Dad— the highly professional, detached father who showed up at the head of the table only on Sundays and holidays. With the life and death demands of a heart surgeon's schedule, it was challenging to create a lifestyle that honored my family priority. I just made it my policy to keep my work schedule clear during the dinner hour. There were times it couldn't be avoided, but for the most part, my family knew they could count on me. Mary made it possible for me to experience a full family life while fulfilling my obligations at the hospital.

> *I grew up with a mom who was always at home. She was a traditional housewife and mother . . . always extremely supportive of Dad. She was there through thick and thin, taking care of the family. Her favorite saying was, "My job is to shine his armor and send him off on his well-fed white horse."*
>
> ~ *Jeff Reed*

We played a lot of basketball in the backyard during visits from Uncle Jay and his family at Thanksgiving. I remember building campfires, and telling stories, especially when we were very young. Dad always bought the largest Christmas tree he could find. I hand-built a stand that could handle those huge trees when I was in high school.

~ Bryan Reed

$\mathcal{B}$y the time I had completed six years at the University of Kansas Hospital, I was eligible to do a sabbatical to advance my career. So in 1967, we moved to Edinburgh, Scotland, so I could do heart research for a year at The Royal Infirmary. I moved over ahead of Mary and the boys so I could find us a place to live, and leased a small stucco cottage with two bedrooms. I purchased a couple floor heaters and plugged them in so it would be warm and toasty when my family arrived.

Mary got us settled into life in the Highlands. She tried new foods from the market and outfitted the boys in kilts for special occasions. Jeff, who managed to develop a wee brogue, was the front man for the family whenever tourists asked for a picture of our adorably Scottish-looking lads. It was a remarkable time for us as a young family, one of hope and adventure. We adjusted fairly well to our new surroundings, although Mary could never get used to the damp cold. Those space heaters were set on high and kept running three seasons of that year. A Scottish friend, David Wade, later described a visit to our home as "subtropical" thanks to Mary's uncompromised position on thermostat setting. He said the only other time he'd ever been so warm was during his tour of duty with General Montgomery in North Africa.

The Atlantic in Winter

Lend me your light
For just a while
The world today
Is hard to see
Where we are going
And why are we there
Walking in darkness
Is so hard to bear
Hold up the glow
To drive away the gloom
Seeing is brilliant
And now filling the room.

~ William Reed, 1967
(written shipboard on the way to Scotland)

*O*nce back in the states, I returned to my position as Associate Professor of Surgery at the University of Kansas Medical Center in Kansas City, Kansas. Mary stayed home as full-time mom. She was great with the boys, taking them to parks, museums and school events. Mary was effusive in her love of our boys, of course. I would often tell the boys I loved them, but I wasn't overtly affectionate. I was there to help with school work and engage in some playful wrestling. Disciplining the boys was a shared duty, but Jeff says the buck stopped with me. "My parents shared discipline equally. My mom would step up more because he had so much on his plate, but my dad had the final authority. I was the one who didn't make good grades and got in trouble. Mom would deal with me, but she'd tell Dad everything," Jeff said.

There weren't hard and fast rules, not even a curfew, but there were clear expectations. Not reaching the mark was "damned by faint praise," as the old saying goes. I wasn't the yelling type . . . it was my style to simply say do you really think that's the thing to do? I look at parenting this way: there have to be some basic rules. Your kids cannot be guests in your home. They have to be responsible for chores. They have to look out for each other. And my boys always knew if they had a problem they could come to me.

As the boys got older, the challenges got bigger. Jeff jumped the traces more than the other two. One time when he was about sixteen, already sporting a beard and weighing in at 180 pounds of pure muscle, something Jeff did stretched my patience too thin. I shook him by the arms until I felt my own shoulders dislocating with the effort. I remember thinking I had to find a different way to make a point with this kid. Jeff called it "playing wall-ball" with him. It became clear to both of us that he had gotten too big to be pushed up against the wall. As the biggest and wildest of my boys, Jeff's adventures were regular fodder for the nurses who waited for me to share the latest installment every Monday morning.

Dr. Reed talked about his family a lot. Once when his boys were little, he took them to see that movie Shampoo, *which was pretty racy at the time. Apparently, during the infamous opening scene that featured glow in the dark prophylactics, his son Bryan asked loudly, "What are they doing, Daddy?"*

Everybody in the movie theater burst out laughing. He told the boys not to tell their mom where he'd taken them. Later that day when he came back from a run, all three boys were sitting around Mary regaling her with a blow by blow description of the movie. Boy, he got in trouble with the wife then! But the Jeff stories were the best . . . the parties when some girl's panties were left under the piano—always some adventure. Or the time Jeff was fussing with his dad outside and Dr. Reed finally manually picked him up and threw him over the hedge.

~ Elaine Russell, RN, Reed's longtime scrub nurse

Bryan could be a bit of a maverick at times, but it never amounted to much. One night he did give us a scare. He'd excused himself to bed at 10:30, but when Mary got up in the middle of the night to check on him—a bit of mother's intuition prompting her—Bryan was gone. He'd jimmied the alarm and gone out raising cain with friends. To his credit, Bryan never drank or got into serious mischief, or if he did, at least he never came home drunk or in trouble. About the worse thing Bryan ever did was throwing all the chairs in the pool at the country club after hours. We did get a call about that. He had to go fish them out the next day.

Martin, our youngest, watched his brothers closely and avoided their mistakes. He recognized his life of privilege, but Martin always saw himself as a typical kid and he saw me as an entirely normal dad. "Dad was there for dinner pretty much every night. He really never isolated himself. He may have had a bad day but didn't let it show to us kids. He'd take us on vacations. I was very fortunate. We went skiing in Colorado every year, and fly fishing in Alaska and Central America. Those were incredible experiences, looking back, but I didn't feel in any way special. It was a regular childhood as far as I was concerned."

What I tried to do, and it became a habit, was to be very efficient with what I was doing medically with patients. That allowed me more time with my family, where my love directed me. Doing things as a family was a retreat from the pressures of my work. We'd go to see the Kansas City Chiefs and KU basketball. There was always a busy schedule of activities around the boys' interests and school events. We went to the Country Club where most of our neighbors and the boys' friends hung out, and we took family ski vacations and trips to visit family in Indiana.

I had many "how could this be happening to me?" moments prompted by experiences and material possessions that I never could have imagined as a boy. As my income increased, in some ways we felt more and more like foreigners in our own world. The only way to consciably deal with the excess was to use it to help others. Sharing what we had was how we got comfortable within the world of the wealthy; that goal evolved to the establishment of a family foundation and, eventually, endowing many different charitable and educational causes. Growing up poor made me keenly aware of the needs of those who were doing without. I've never forgotten what it felt like to be one of them.

Mary and I both felt awkward with the social status that came with wealth. Considering our family backgrounds, neither of us ever felt entirely at ease with the moneyed crowd. Mary never needed diamonds or fur coats. That just wasn't who she was. The first time we took the family skiing, Mary remarked that, "These are not our kind of people." I told her the only thing that was important to me was right there in that car. Even after we started raising horses, our approach was down-to-earth and family-focused. Horseracing was something we could enjoy as a family.

While our financial position afforded such opportunities, we have always remained very much a traditional Midwestern family with small town values. I have been an ordinary dad who rakes his own leaves then tips over in the ashcan while stomping them down. "Dad was goofy and funny," Martin said. It is a source of such pride to me that Dr. William Reed, pioneering heart surgeon and Director of Cardiovascular Diseases at a major metropolitan hospital, was just plain old Dad to his sons.

My approach to life outside of work made the hospital brass nervous on more than one occasion. On one of the ski trips, I cracked some ribs. Then there was the time I broke my wrist and couldn't do surgery for six weeks—the result of the aforementioned leaf-stomping debacle during which I stuck out my arm to break my fall. I did embellish that story whenever possible with tales of jumping from a helicopter to save a drowning victim, but I'm not sure anyone at work found that at all humorous. Nor were they amused by a close call in my own farm pond. I was strapped into a fishing float-tube that flipped over when I leaned too far in the direction of a fish I was reeling in. If Martin hadn't come to the rescue, the drowning victim would have been me.

> *Dad loved a good fire. When we cleared the land for Stonecrest Farm, he'd have a brush pile blazing so huge that people saw the smoke and called the fire department. This happened on more than one occasion. It actually got to be a joke around the neighborhood. One particularly memorable burn left a tree stump that was unmistakably phallic shaped. Dad left it stand in tribute. That's my dad. He's definitely a boys' dad. To this day, if they cut to a shot of the Denver Bronco cheerleaders, both of my sons yell WHOA the same way their papa always did.*
>
> *~ Jeff Reed*

> *My daddy is just human and a dad. Out of nowhere he'll come up with something rude and crass, but funny. He has little idiosyncrasies. He likes bread at every meal—breakfast, lunch and dinner. It's his little thing. He has a specific brown-checkered robe only worn on Christmas mornings. When we went to brunch after church on Sunday, if toast didn't come with the bacon and eggs he ordered, he would sit there until it arrived. It's a gene that he has.*
>
> *~ Martin Reed*

According to my partner, Bill Hamaker, I "had a penchant for doing things that got (me) into trouble." That's probably an exaggeration, but I do enjoy mowing my own lawn, clearing brush with a tractor, and doing all the handyman work around the house. Doing ordinary things is familiar to me; it keeps me grounded. My background being what it was, my mind was programmed to do things for myself.

Dad and Mom took us skiing in Colorado, and on trips to see relatives in Indiana. Some of my favorite times were fly fishing trips with my dad. We went to some incredible places—Montana and Wyoming in the American West, Labrador, Central America. Alaska was hard to beat because it was such a primitive, untouched frontier and we were able to fish for many different species. Those trips were about fly fishing all day with shore lunches of freshly caught trout followed by grilled halibut for dinner. Evenings were spent plotting the next day's excursions, cleaning fly lines, shoring up fly boxes, and replaying the often embellished stories of the day. Interesting how much fish grow from their catch and release on a sunny afternoon to when they are recalled over supper that same night. Martin and I would occasionally descend into our somewhat inaccurate vocal renditions of favorite fishing trip songs such as Gordon Lightfoot's "The Wreck of the Edmund Fitzgerald." Dad would tolerate these ramblings in good order but he was not one to participate . . . only observe.

~ Bryan Reed

Once we were on a vacation to Hawaii and they booked us into a room overlooking the highway instead of the oceanview Dad had reserved. He kept his cool like he always does, but that front desk manager was squirming. When Bill Reed says calmly, "Help me understand how this happened," you are about to be engaged in a negotiation with a man who is not going to back down. You might as well give up right at the git-go, because you're going down. I mean when I'm mad, I rage. Dad is just the opposite. He gets quiet. Without a word, you know something is terribly wrong. In the few arguments my parents have had, I've watched my dad just get quiet and not say anything for days.

~ Jeff Reed

$\mathcal{I}$t wasn't easy being the doctor's perfect wife, and Mary had to get away from the pressure once in a while. One of her favorite retreats was a week at a spa where she'd be totally pampered and didn't have to lift a finger. She would usually take someone with her—my sister or, later, one of our daughters-in-law. She'd come back and tell me about some guy there who would pour out his heart to her, how she'd listen. Men were often attracted to Mary, but she was never, ever flirtatious. I never had a moment of doubt about her. Mary didn't have a total appreciation for how beautiful she was. She would dress to the nines and I was so proud to walk into a restaurant with her and the boys. She'd turn heads; she was a knockout. It was a matter of pride for me that people would look at her, yet she was never a "hey, look at me" girl.

Those three little boys and their mother meant the world to me. They still do, except, of course, my sons are not little anymore. They all have wives and children of their own. My family was and is my foundation. Everything I aspired to and achieved professionally was possible because I was grounded by Mary and my boys. Thinking back on the early years, it seems idyllic that I had a beautiful wife and three wonderful sons to come home to each night after work, but that's what I remember most happily about that time of my life. There were days when the cost of living was so high in terms of my physical and emotional endurance that I don't know how I would have made it without them.

Mary dedicated her life to me and the children. I have felt selfish that she has always gone in whatever direction that I wanted to go. Was it ok to expect that of her? She never protested. Her love has been unconditional . . . is that a voluntary thing or a gift one is born with? It's so self-regarding and ego-centric . . . doing my thing because Mary makes that possible. She's always felt that she loved me more than I loved her. On our wedding day, there she was, this exceptional woman—the most beautiful I've ever been around—incandescent with happiness. And Mary is as beautiful on the inside as she is on the outside. I've been the lucky guy who got to be married to someone like that . . . to experience that kind of devotion, and to know that it made my professional success possible.

> *Dad received a lot of awards and recognition, but he never, ever stepped into that spotlight solo. He always pulled my mom into the light with him. He never took credit for his accomplishments without acknowledging her. My mother had a really successful career herself before having kids; she was a very devoted, educated nurse and nursing instructor. She'd have been fine with that as a career, but somewhere along the line, she decided it was time to stay home and be a mother and wife. Back then my folks weren't wealthy by any means, but it was a decision they made together. I don't think she ever regrets it.*
>
> *~ Jeff Reed*

There have been times I've felt I didn't deserve Mary or haven't done right by her, often with good cause. I still don't know what to do with that feeling. Sometimes it follows me like a shadow as I walk through the door of our home that's full of her warmth and style and sound—literally. Mary has a habit of setting each clock ahead or behind the hour by just a few minutes so that we can hear and enjoy the chimes of each individual one. That's what Mary is like . . . magical. She loves completely. That is one of my deficiencies, in a romantic sense.

What is the expectation of the person giving the unconditional love? Reciprocity? I think Mary might say my love was conditional—

that she had to perform perfectly to be worthy. I certainly never felt that way. Her idea of having to be perfect for me—what she thought my expectations for her were—I hope I didn't put that on her. She had to be feeling a lot of pressure about the role she played, a doctor's wife, relative to her childhood training, the era and society. Maybe she stills does.

> *I think Mary began her life with Bill with the expectation that she had to perform perfectly to be acceptable as his wife and the mother of his children. That stemmed from her relationship with her father, in my opinion. Bill's professional life took both of them along a certain path that gave Mary the opportunity, in addition to being a loving mother, to do what she wanted to do most: generously nurture the charitable endeavors they have endowed . . . all her loving philanthropies. She has always enjoyed doing the good things that his work made possible. I know Mary has always loved being Mrs. William Reed, the mother of their three fine sons, and a devoted grandmother.*
>
> *~ Jo Jeanne Callaway, MD, Psychiatrist and family friend*

There have been ups and downs in our marriage; my biggest regrets in life are the downs. I can be distant and inaccessible. My tendency to clam up when I'm upset is hard to live with . . . I guess my boys have commented on "the silent treatment." The upside of it is that I know I was trying not to make things worse by saying something that would be hurtful, something I'd regret. We can forgive but rarely do we forget such things. I'd like to think I was sparing them by saying nothing at all. They might not see it that way. Maybe I'm making a grand rationalization. Believe me, there have been plenty of times I've had to apologize for being childish like that. Mary has put up with a lot.

Perhaps I am painting Mary too one-dimensionally. She has always had her own mind, calling the shots as she saw them. No one is perfect, not even Mary, and she would be the first to admit it. The truth is that she could be over-protective of the boys, particularly Martin, and possessive with me. If she thought a woman was getting too friendly with me at a cocktail party, Mary would filet her with a look while sending me off to refill her glass or some such errand that marked me as her property. She was the queen, or maybe general is a better descriptor. Three days prior to a dinner party hosted at our house, I'd come home from work and throw my hat in ahead of me to see if it got shot at before risking entry myself. As much as she loved entertaining, the preparations she waged for a big event brought pending warfare to mind rather than a pleasant evening. The boys and I would lay low until it was time to greet our guests with uniform smiles. Everything had to be exactly right. I wish her father could have seen it . . . he might finally have given her a nod of approval. Many times, I sensed that was her real agenda, and I wondered if Mary was conscious of this.

Regardless, for better or for worse, we built a life on the foundation of ourselves. I want to be sure to express that if I had been married to a different person, I'm not sure what happened would have happened in terms of what I've been able to accomplish. Mary carried her part of the ball. She always had the home warm and receptive when I returned. She parented solo much of the time because I couldn't be there for everything whereas she simply had to be there. Of course, Mary has always been her own person with her own projects and passions. On top of everything else, she managed an apartment complex that we bought up near the hospital so there'd be an affordable place for medical students and others just starting out in life to live safely in the city. Our residents loved her like a house mother because she mothered them in loving ways—not at all like a typical landlord.

Mary participated in every major decision of our lives and we steered this thing together. Sometimes we weren't on the same page. You work things out, you find a way. I think we'd both agree that there's more to be proud of than sorry for in our relationship. That song, "No one knows what goes on behind closed doors" says a lot of what a husband and wife shouldn't have to explain to anybody but themselves.

> *Whenever my father-in-law is feeling down, she's there. It's been an incredible model for our relationship for over thirty years. Jeff and I learned how to be married from witnessing his parents' marriage.*
>
> ~ Rita Reed, Jeff's wife

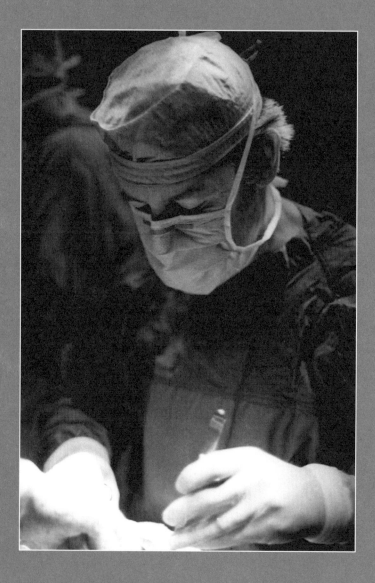

Dr. Reed performing surgery in the 1970s.

CHAPTER 5

Surgeon

Nature arms each man with some

faculty which enables him to do easily

some feat impossible to any other

~ *Ralph Waldo Emerson*

Can any of us truly enter "Into the labyrinth of another's being," as Yeats put it? At first, I thought I wanted to do this, so I had set my sights on psychiatry. Living and working at Norways was an invaluable experience that increased my sensitivity to aspects of health and healing that have to do with the relationship between the emotional and physical states.

In the 1950s, there were large institutions for people with mental problems, and I briefly had a job at one of them, the Indiana State Hospital for the Insane. I interviewed each patient, asking basic questions to determine whether they were delusional or psychotic. Then I would make an appraisal of his or her mental state. For three months, I talked to these people who hadn't seen a family member or the outside world for years. How could you not be crazy? It was a heartbreaking experience, and ever since, I have always felt sensitized to the many factors contributing to the emotional state of my patient. The state of mind has inestimable influence on wellness and the recovery process.

After my stint at the state hospital, I started an internship in July 1954 at the University of Kansas. My experience with mentally ill patients was invaluable and fascinating to me, but as I've said, my military status was such that I could have been called back to active duty. I felt that a surgical discipline might be more useful to the military than psychiatric training. But the war ended and the military wasn't calling anyone up, so my obligation no longer seemed imminent. By July 1955, it was clear I wouldn't have to go back.

During my internship I found I really loved the surgical rotations. I had a feel for it—with both hands, in fact. I discovered I was ambidextrous in the OR—I could use instruments or cut and tie with either hand (not the case elsewhere). I decided to focus on that discipline and gave up the idea of psychiatric training at Menninger's. The program at KU was approved for four residents in general surgery each year, and I would have been the fifth. Dr. Frank Allbritten was chair of surgery then. He saw enough promise in me to make an exception, so I was given an opportunity to join the surgical training program. During my second year, I was required to do a rotation in the animal research laboratory. My mentors there were Dr. Paul Schloerb and Dr. Fred Kittle.

Dr. Kittle was the head of cardiothoracic surgery. He was a talented intellectual who played classical piano and had a collection of books on surgical history. Fred Kittle took me under his wing, bringing me along to national meetings; he would introduce me to the pioneers in cardiac surgery, many of whom were his friends and peers. He was an inspiration to me. One year he gave me a Christmas present that was a large book on surgical history by Dr. Francis Moore of Johns Hopkins. He inscribed it "in esteem" with a note on the inside cover. I still have that in a place of honor.

I knew Bill Reed before I met him in person. I heard stories from some of my classmates who were lucky enough to have assisted him in surgery when he was a young resident at KUMC. On one occasion, he was assisting the senior cardiovascular surgeon in an operation on a little girl under six years old who had a hole in her heart. When the senior surgeon started to close the incision in the heart, putting the edges of the incised tissue back together, he didn't get them approximated exactly as they'd been separated. That's important because if the tissue is not realigned the way it came apart, it will form greater scar tissue. So I heard that this Dr. Reed had first said very quietly, "Doctor, I believe that stitch is going to need redoing." But the head cardiovascular surgeon paid no attention. Then Dr. Reed more emphatically, but politely, said, "Dr. Smith, I believe that suture is going to have to be taken out." He was still ignored. The third time, I heard that Dr. Reed had said bluntly and with authority, "Dr. Smith, take that suture out and re-do it!" Then the chief surgeon finally did exactly that. I just loved hearing that account of what my fellow medical student saw firsthand in the OR. What it said to me was that Dr. Reed cared most about the little patient's scarred heart. He cared so much that he challenged the head of the cardiovascular department, a political risk indeed, but one that I profoundly admired.

~ Jo Jeanne Callaway, MD, Psychiatrist

It was surprising how much I drew from my high school vocational classes at times, at least conceptually. Machine shop taught me a lot about why things break down and how innovation is often the key to fixing them. A machinist's mentality has its applications for a doctor, particularly in cardiac surgery because what we were doing in those early days was so new and sometimes right from the hip.

Before we had all the technology we've got today, surgery was a multisensory experience. Even listening was involved because we didn't have echocardiograms. I'd rely on what I was hearing through the stethoscope to tell me which heart valve was leaking and how bad. With practice, you'd develop a feel of the procedure; you'd gain muscle memory of what you needed to do. I did operations of all kinds for a number of years so by the time I was focused on cardiothoracic surgery I had a surgeon's feel for every part of the body. That was a tremendous advantage—to see the whole in context to its parts and vice versa.

I learned to avoid trouble by staying out of trouble in the first place. When I was facing something in heart surgery that was really unusual that I'd not done before and didn't have any visual resource to go to, I'd read about it then consult others who might have something to contribute. After the surgery, I'd make a clay model of that heart and its abnormalities to show at our cardiovascular conference. As a teaching tool, it provided a three dimensional view of the situation. It seems primitive by today's standards, but it was a great advantage in those days.

$\mathcal{L}$n 1954, heart surgery was still in its infancy. We were all figuring things out by dire necessity and it was largely unregulated. It was a risky time in a pioneering field of medicine. There was a huge price to be paid, and doctors like DeBakey, Cooley, Kirklin, and Barnard paved the way for all of us. Norman Shumway did things that no one thought could be done at the time. The early leaders in cardiac surgery possessed a deep conviction for the goal of safe open heart surgery. They sacrificed their personal lives and even professional reputations in some cases. Many internalized each failure but recovered sufficiently to move forward with the cause.

In those days, we were anesthetizing patients then inducing profound hypothermia—cooling the body down to thirty degrees centigrade with slushed ice water. When the body temperature is that cold, the brain is protected for a period of time. We'd get the patient on the operating table, open the chest and try to fix the heart. At normal temperature, you could work like this for about three minutes, but when the body is that cold with no blood flowing to the brain, you've extended that window up to eight to ten minutes max.

There was so much working against us in those early days. We didn't even realize that you couldn't sew a patient up with air bubbles still inside him, that's how new it was. It was very much hit or miss. We were figuring things out as we went. Today, we take for granted a lot of what was not known then about how to take over the heart's function while it was stopped down for repairs or replacement. Something had to keep the blood flowing through the body while adding oxygen and removing carbon dioxide during a heart operation. In 1953, Dr. John H. Gibbon at the Jefferson Medical College in Philadelphia invented the first heart-lung machine, but it cost about a million dollars which made it unfeasible for most hospitals in those days. As the saying goes, necessity is the mother of invention, so we kept innovating and problem-solving. This is how we moved forward.

> *Reed was the doctor to watch. He was such a pioneer in his field.*
>
> *~ Betty Keim, formerly with the*
> *Kansas Hospital Authority Board*

It became apparent that success would depend on our ability to organize a team of individuals, recognizing each one's unique expertise. Specialization was essential, but working as a unit was critical. This was a shift in thinking—to place value on a team approach instead of everyone supporting the lead role of just one strong individual's function (and usually personality): the cardiac surgeon.

This philosophy made sense to me. I recognized how crucial it was to affirm the importance of each person in that operating room, and by extension, everyone whose contribution was making it possible for us to save a life, from the scrub nurse to the janitor. As a valued member of the team, every one of us with passion for this work shared the credit and the thrill of a successful outcome. I felt strongly that this was how to get the best results, and I have devoted myself to this approach to medicine.

*T*he first open heart surgery at the University of Kansas Medical Center (KUMC) was on September 26, 1956. Dr. Frederick Kittle repaired a little five year old boy's heart. As a member of the surgical house staff, I was on the team, and my job was to operate the heart-lung machine. Unlike Gibbon's high-priced equipment, we would be using a bubble oxygenator comprised of plastic food tubing—a cost-effective innovation developed by Dr. Richard Dewall at the University of Minnesota.

For six months, I had been doing research in the lab in preparation for the case. What we learned in those research experiments frequently came into the operating room via the trial and error type of clinical progress. I brought over the pump and oxygenator from the Wahl Dog Lab to the main OR at midnight. I wanted to have it all set up for the operation that was to start at eight in the morning. I felt confident from the work I had done in the lab, and was excited to be a part of the team. It just didn't occur to me that we wouldn't succeed. We all felt the pressure but also a powerful sense of readiness.

The small child on the operating table had light brown hair, as I recall. He seemed kind of skinny, but then an operating table has a way of emphasizing the frailty of whoever is lying on it. My eyes swiveled between the equipment and the little boy it was keeping alive. The machines blipped and hummed, the feeling in the room was electric. Everyone was focused intently, hovering right on the edge of every possible thing he or she would need to do next . . . ready for anything, at least we all hoped so. That little boy's name was Roger, and he survived, which was a great success, but equally profound was what happened after that.

Our next heart repair patient died, and then the next . . . and the next. In total, we had nine fatalities following that first successful heart operation. We just didn't know the mistakes we were making. Dr. Kittle, who was the surgeon on all of them, took each one hard. The emotional toll on everyone in the department was so high, and we were keenly aware of the grief of all those families. I began to question whether I had what it took to do this work. I told Mary I thought maybe cardio-thoracic surgery wasn't my calling. Her encouragement was my lifeline. Heart surgery was the only hope for survival for these patients so we had to keep trying.

By 1956, I was a general surgery resident with a reputation for working fast. In those days, speed was as important as skill, particularly in heart surgery and that's where my aspirations were. You could be the best surgeon ever to grace the planet, but your patient could still die if you weren't fast enough. The minute that patient was hooked up to the heart and lung machine, the heart stopped and every moment you were racing against death. After surgery, heart patients were sent to a general recovery room—we didn't even have Intensive Care Units back then—and a lot of patients didn't recover. We had to find out what we were doing wrong so we could start doing it right.

The earliest versions of a heart-lung machine were primitive compared to today's technology. The challenge was to oxygenate the blood without air getting into the heart chamber, which could create an embolism. I spent hundreds of hours in research and on the development of oxygenators trying to discover why some of our patients never woke up after heart surgery even though everything seemed to have gone well. I suspected something could be wrong with our attempts to oxygenate the blood, and then created an experiment to prove it. I applied a red dye to the anti-foam we were using to break down the oxygenated blood bubbles to their liquid state. This allowed me to track where it was in the body. In post-mortem analysis of the animals after surgery, I saw that anti-foam was present in the brain tissue of the animals—definitely not where it was supposed to be. I believed this was causing blockage in the small blood vessels of the brain resulting in a stroke or possibly death. So then I focused my efforts on developing an oxygenator that worked without anti-foam. Ultimately, this helped us develop much safer blood oxygenating equipment, and that led to more lives being saved.

In 1959, I was senior resident and the only cardiothoracic surgery resident at University of Kansas Medical Center. I was directly responsible for dying patients whose only hope was our team. Since the risks were so high, I had to get the next-of-kin signature on a post mortem permit before we started the surgery. Setting the stage realistically with a family that their loved one might not survive, I would then have to ask their permission to explore why the surgery didn't work. We needed a signed release form before we began so we could do an autopsy on the spot, if necessary, and discover anything we could about what caused the patient's death. It was an excruciating conversation to have, especially while trying to convey a sense of hope and optimism with the family.

> *Open heart surgery was very difficult to do back then because you had to make a heart stop beating then keep it alive. This hadn't been done successfully in very many centers before Dr. Reed began his work. In the Fifties, the earliest heart-lung machines were being used in patients, and in the early Sixties, the first attempts at bypassing diseased coronary arteries were performed. Compared to today's standards, the best machines available were still crude, so you had to be extremely adept as a surgeon . . . to work rapidly sewing the grafts on the heart with minute little stitches in a tiny hole in an artery. Sutures tied too loosely led to major bleeding into the chest and possible catastrophes in the ICU later; tied too tightly, the flow through the graft to the heart would be cut off to create a heart attack. There was little to no margin for error. Success depended on precision, speed and outstanding judgment. You simply had to have a gift and Bill Reed had those gifts. Even in the latter phase of his career, Bill would be done with*

three cases when others were finishing two. He began cardiac surgery when swift work was a necessity and he maintained that superior pace even when younger, highly skilled surgeons worked at slower speeds. I told him he was a mutant . . . in favorable ways that made him so successful.

~ Charles Porter, MD, Cardiologist

He has no unnecessary movement with his hands. Every movement was purposeful and that's what made him so good.

~ Elaine Russell, RN

When I finished my training in June 1960, I joined the surgical faculty at the University of Kansas Hospital. In the fall of that year, I faced one of the toughest operations I had done to date. A toddler who drank some oven cleaner out of a bottle he found under the kitchen sink was rushed into the ER with his frantic parents. I was on call, and I'd not encountered anything like this before. The toxic liquid had destroyed the esophagus—the tube leading from the mouth down to the stomach. By the time this little guy got into my operating room, he was in critical condition, which was often what happened in those cases back then.

I remembered reading about an experimental procedure, and I'd seen a short movie clip at a medical conference showing something I thought might work. However, I didn't know anyone personally who'd done this, and there wasn't time to consult anybody anyway. I had to figure it out on my own on the spot. I had to try to save that baby. So I removed a section of his large bowel, cleaned it, and fashioned an esophagus from it. It was a delicate operation that had to result in something strong enough to hold up through the swallow-function right where the new tube was going to be attached to what was left of his esophagus. I'm happy to report that it worked. That little fellow survived and grew up to become the award-winning American playwright, James Still.

Decades later, the *Kansas City Star* did a story that got some national coverage on this, prompted by Still's attempts to find me and thank me for his life. Many patients or their family members have contacted me over the years to thank me for the role I've played at a critical point in their life. It is deeply humbling to have the opportunity to participate in someone's life in this way, but I'm acutely aware that I am just one of the team with an entire hospital behind it that deserves to share in that moment of gratitude.

At first, my focus was on fixing the kind of heart problems that children were born with—known as "congenital" heart abnormalities. It took a cool head and calm hand to open up a child's chest. Kids can die quickly; those surgeries were not usually as straightforward. You encounter congenital abnormalities that require instant innovation. I would approach each patient as a unique challenge. With little girls, I would make an incision along the lines where her bathing suit top would be one day, so she wouldn't have a big scar in the middle along the sternum below the Adam's apple down to her belly. I figured they would appreciate that later.

I enjoyed this work because I love children, but the pressure was unrelenting. Trying to add some years onto an already long, full adult life is one thing, but with kids, you're doing everything possible to just to save a life that's hardly begun. It wasn't always possible. When a little one dies, it's difficult to find any consolation. Day-in and day-out, the weight of that can be almost unbearable.

So I learned to play hurt, to soldier on, to be the kind of professional that the situation required of me because in those early days I was closer to pulling that off than anyone else. Mary gently reminded me of this every time I wanted to quit. She'd say, "You are who needs to be there." So I went back and tried again. Let me tell you, after you've been up for three days straight, catching only quick snatches of sleep on a gurney beside a patient, you begin to ask yourself if it's worth it—even if you are the one who's needed.

One of those dark stretches still haunts me. Over the course of two days in the early spring of 1960, a sweet, beautiful twelve year old named Scarlett was slowly dying and I couldn't help her. She looked normal in every way on the outside, as though she could bounce out of that hospital bed and race off to school. But Scarlett had pulmonary valvular stenosis restricting the flow of blood to her lungs. Her anxious parents watched her get weaker and weaker as she grew, not keeping up with the other kids at recess, eventually unable to climb stairs, and finally not even maintaining normal activities on a small scale. Here was a girl fading from life just as it was beginning to bloom. I was the resident in training and scrubbed up to assist the surgeon in the operating room. We did everything we knew how to do back then, but it wasn't enough. Nowadays, Scarlett's condition can be fixed with a pulmonary valvotomy, a routine operation with very little risk.

After the surgery, I spent the next two and a half days in the recovery room watching Scarlett not recover. She was slipping away and I didn't know how to keep her alive. Nothing I tried succeeded. Mary was working at the hospital in those days, so she witnessed this firsthand, experiencing the anguish and despair as much as I did. It was such a helpless feeling to watch that girl die—it went against every instinct I had about how life should work and what I thought should happen. At that time in heart surgery, there were so many more questions than answers. Physicians were the answer-people, yet we didn't have the right ones for Scarlett. It shook me to the core, which I believe is a thing that happens to every physician at some point early in his or her career. All these ideals we hold about what we are capable of come crashing down around us. I wasn't a solid rock for Scarlett's family to stand on, although I tried my best to maintain a brave face. Thankfully, I could let down my reserve and genuinely feel the pain of this tragedy in Mary's presence.

Such things take the measure of a man . . . whether he can stand up under crippling strain and exhaustion when he's too emotionally drained to conceive of the sun ever rising again. I limped away from that case completely unsure that I was the man for this job. I grieved that girl's death deeply. Mary kept me together, and a sense of duty brought me back.

There is no way to avoid the strain and pain, one simply learns to cope. Fortunately, we learned from our mistakes and began to see more success. Eventually, with experience and new technologies, we discovered a lot of what we didn't know. We got better at fixing the problems and even transplanting the heart. Patients survived more often.

In the 1960s, heart disease was in an epidemic stage. The first Surgeon General's report on cigarette smoking as a cause was not presented until 1964. Uncontrolled cholesterol level was not commonly measured and often ran well over 300, compared to today's norms at 200 or less. Cardiology was in it's infancy. Thanks to angiography, we learned that a heart attack was caused by a freshly formed clot and not by a slowly closing cholesterol clogged artery—but that wouldn't be discovered until the 1970s.

It was an era typified by high stakes trial and error. Mortality was about twelve to fifteen out of one hundred, yet Bill Reed had done a hundred consecutive aortic valve replacements with no fatalities, which nobody else had done. Bill never squawked about the workload. It was good to look at a case with him because he'd never talk about what was going to be difficult for him, you only heard him discuss how he would find success.

~ Charles Porter, MD, Cardiologist

When I had nothing to give

I reached out to find a way

What I discovered, what I learned, how I changed

Helping God heal the sick

was a great privilege

A blessing opened by heart

to share with others

everything I had to give

seemed to grow with

the giving . . . and I grew

~ William Reed

He was such a pioneer. I feel so privileged to know him from those days. I first met him when I moved to Kansas. As a nurse at Allegheny General Hospital back in Pennsylvania, I had observed open heart surgery one time. I was really interested in seeing more of that, and Reed was the doctor to watch.

~ Betty Keim, formerly with the
Kansas Hospital Authority Board

*I*n my mind, I was always rehearsing a surgical procedure, staying focused, preparing. Very often in my sleep, I would come up with something I hadn't thought about before. Somehow the thing I'd been puzzling over would come to me in a dream.

I remember operating on small girl I'd already repaired previously; that meant there would be scar tissue to get through—often the heart is stuck to the backside of the breastbone with layers of it. When you open the breastbone or sternum you have to be careful not to also cut into the heart in such cases, particularly when the chest cavity is as tiny as a child's. The patient can bleed to death in a few moments. Mentally, I safely fixed that little girl's heart a hundred times before the actual surgery. I'd wake up disoriented by dreaming that I was doing the operation in the middle of a plowed field where I hoed weeds as a kid. But in that dreaming, something might come to me; I would know to insert my finger as a barrier between the heart and the saw—a fairly unorthodox and risky practice, but an effective one that I continued to use the rest of my career.

You sleep when you can, and hope for those dreams when working around the clock. I could work thirty-six hours straight all the way into my seventies. I trained myself to do so. Everyone did. I'd have cases all day, be home for dinner with my family, and then back to the hospital for a night call. The next day would be fully booked, too. Nowadays, doctors fill in for each other and residents only work set hours. It didn't used to be that way, and, personally, I think it has cost us some quality assurance to lose that continuity with a patient, not to mention the dreamtime.

I was doing my psychiatry residency when I woke up one morning with an acute bowel obstruction. I went to x-ray and was told I had a massive growth around my small intestine needing surgical removal. I asked Bill Reed if he would do the procedure.

Assisted by a gynecological surgeon, he found that the blood supply to my right ovary had been compromised by a prior experimental surgical procedure. The starving ovarian tissue had attached itself to and grown around my small intestine. I had been unable to get pregnant because of that procedure, done before medical school on the basis of a misdiagnosis.

I didn't know that this surgical history related to my small bowel obstruction, but Bill Reed figured it all out on the spot. Because he was a good friend, Bill had long known how much I had wanted a family. Now, as my doctor, he understood why. He cleaned up the mess my reproductive anatomy had become. The next morning, he checked on me, and said, "Jo Jeanne, I think you'll get pregnant now." I laughed and said, "Bill, I'll bet you do first!"

I was already thirty-eight years old, but one year later I was pregnant, carried my baby to term, and was in my hospital room at St. Luke's, where by now both Bill and I were on the hospital staff, awaiting my C-section. Bill strode into my hospital room, sat down and with a big smile on his face said, "You know, this baby is part mine!" And he was right. He deserved much credit for my son's existence because without his surgical expertise outside his specialty, my baby's birth the following morning never would have happened.

~ Jo Jeanne Callaway, MD, Psychiatrist

*A*pparently, I had a reputation for suffering no fools in my operating room. That was probably well deserved. Some wouldn't scrub with me because my expectations were more than they were up to at the time. The challenge for my scrub team was to be competent as well as fast. My scrub nurse for over two decades was Elaine Russell, although I knew her right from the start of her career when her last name was still Hollenbeck. She came to us fresh off the family farm in Missouri after she finished nursing school. Elaine was an amazing "skirt"—that's what we called a scrub nurse back then—and she was a lot of fun to boot.

> *I stood beside Dr. Reed, handing the instruments in surgery for twenty years. We would do an entire case and he wouldn't once have to tell me what he needed. I just knew. I didn't have that mindmeld with any other surgeon. Many people watching us were in awe.*

> *Of course, I can recall handing him the usual suture once and he surprised me by asking for something different. I hesitated a moment so he looked up over his glasses and said, "Humor me," with a little glint in his eye.*

> *Many people found him intimidating, his standards were so high. He commanded so much respect. And his amazing hands—they once put them on the cover of the newspaper.*

> *Reed designed some of the equipment—the aortic cannula, a specialized needle on the sternal wires that he used to wire the chest back together, was his custom design. He could have patented that but he never focused on that part. He was just trying to improve our efforts.*

> *Everything he did was purposeful, and that's what made him so good. We all worked silently, completely focused.*

> *But he could be fun, too. He was the first surgeon to bring music into the OR. He liked John Denver, opera, classical, Judy Collins, Creedence Clearwater Revival. As we closed up*

a successful case, he'd say, "Crank it up." We'd all start singing Jimmy Buffett's "Wasting away again in Margaritaville" once the pressure was off. We were working fools, but we sure had some good times.

~ Elaine Russell, RN

The intensity of surgery makes a close knit group of an OR team. Generally, everyone performed well under pressure. If they couldn't cut it, I'd have to rotate them out after a week or so. I never yelled or threw things like some surgeons do when things get tense. If you were good enough to be on my team, you were treated with care, respect, and trust. We were all focused but would loosen up a bit when we were closing up a successful case. We'd turn up the tunes and the intensity would give way to a more relaxed atmosphere and casual banter. We were colleagues and friends. For years I had an on-going bet on the Kansas City Chiefs game with Dan Dotson, a perfusionist running the heart-lung machine. Come Monday morning, the loser would be looking for creative ways to pay it off. Once it was all in pennies and another time one of us sealed a five dollar bill in a hard cast.

We would have a brief break between cases so I could make my rounds and dictate notes; then we'd get scrubbed and ready for the next case. For years, I'd carry the heaviest caseload—usually three cardiac surgeries a day. My expectations were very high, the pace and performance level could be hard to take. One nurse who was known to be fairly dramatic in her manner waited until her last day of work then walked over to me as I was operating and bit me on the ankle. She said, "I've always wanted to do that, and now you can't fire me." Well, that surprised me, but what could I do? I just kept on operating.

Henry Pearley was one of my main scrub nurses for many years. Elaine always said I wasn't as hard on him as I was on everybody else, to which I countered that the other nurses were perhaps too hard on him. Henry was African American and maybe he reminded me of my childhood best friend Nip, or maybe he was somebody who needed an opportunity and I could relate to that feeling. Either way, I do know that even if Henry was slower, he was accurate, easy going, and full of compassion. If I got impatient, he'd say, "Everything's going to be alright, Chief." And it was.

I had heard about Dr. Reed. I knew he was at St. Luke's, and one day I happened to be walking by Room 11 in the surgical suite, kind of looking in to see what he was doing. Everybody told me I would not be able to go in that room; that I wouldn't be able to work there. The hospital wanted special people working with him, but it turns out I was one of the special people, even though I didn't know that yet.

Dr. Reed waved me in, so I went. I wanted to see what was going on . . . it gave me an incentive to work. From that day on, I started training to work with him. It was the career direction I'd been looking towards for about five years. I had worked with all phases of surgery—obstetrics, ENT, orthopedics, in-utero, all those positions. They all liked the work I was doing, but somehow I thought I'd like cardiovascular surgery better, and that's what I wanted.

I had a hunch Reed had been told by one of the nurses from KU that they were sending a good technician his way, someone who could help move things along. When I went in his surgical suite that first time, it kind of surprised me because he had classical music playing. I loved it and he did, too. He just seemed like a person who you would want to work with. He's one of the teachers, the kind that gives you an incentive to look and see what's going on so you could go ahead and carry out the case.

~ Henry Pearley, RN

Henry Pearley was by my side during one particularly tense case, not that the surgery was more challenging, but the dynamics of it were fairly unprecedented. I'm not sure "VIP" is the right term for this patient, but he was certainly a person of notoriety. He arrived with armed bodyguards who walked right into the OR with guns strapped to their chest. Immediately, I had to take control of that situation, so I calmly told them the people in that room were all safe and there was nothing the bodyguards had to worry about. In fact, what I needed was for them to step outside so we could get started, which they did. That patient did fine and recovered 100 percent, to our great relief.

In his summer whites, the young Dr. Reed with a patient who wrote that he was "the cuttest doctor" on a photo she sent him after getting well, circa 1954.

CHAPTER 6

Dr. Cool

What one has, one ought to use; and whatever he does,

he should do with all his might.

~ Cicero

When you're dealing with people's lives on a daily basis, the pressure can be crushing. The margins are so narrow in heart surgery. It does something to your psyche. A little mistake can kill somebody, and the stress can destroy your health physically and mentally. I was fortunate. It was rare for me to feel any tension at all, and I recognize that as part of the gift I was given to do this work. They gave me the nickname "Dr. Cool." Occasionally, I had cases with people that I knew that gave me "fighter's anxiety" right up until the first incision, but then it went away and I was confident, focused, and on my game.

> *Bill can be very stoic about things. In the OR they called him Dr. Cool because he never raised his voice or showed anxiety or anger. He would just put a finger over an artery spurting with blood and calmly call for a suture. I've never even seen him swear . . . I honestly wish he would.*
>
> *~ Mary Reed*

Surgeons often have a reputation for being Divas in the OR, throwing instruments or chewing somebody out if they get upset, but if I was struggling with a case, no one would know it. Charles Porter claimed, "If Bill Reed was upset with you he'd just talk to you even less than he did before. I never saw him lose his cool . . . just a look, that look." Elaine Russell said I was intimidating when she first met me, "He'd look at you over those half-glasses and you would quiver—oh my God, what did I do wrong? If you weren't fast enough, you'd hear it—a "thwok" sound where he took his middle finger and snapped the center palm of his surgical glove impatiently. You did not want to be the person he had to snap his gloves at!" All I can say to that is she didn't hear that very often.

Elaine came to know a very different side of me after years of working at my side. "Dr. Reed had this marvelous dry sense of humor. He was always teasing me. If I came in without any make-up on, he'd volunteer to call the blood bank and arrange for a transfusion." On Mondays, I'd always want an update on Elaine's weekend—she was quite the social butterfly and popular with the guys. I remember not liking one of her boyfriends at all . . . and sure enough, it didn't last long. I think Elaine would admit that I had very good instincts about that sort of thing.

> *There was only one time I can ever recall Dr. Reed losing his cool, and that was with an OR technician who had some relative high up in hospital administration. This guy thought he was pretty special, and one time he said something incredibly inappropriate to Dr. Reed in a case during closing. Reed ignored him at first, but the guy kept it up. Finally, Reed calmly told him he could leave, and the guy said, "You can't tell me what to do." At that point, Dr. Reed said firmly, "Get out of my operating room." The guy refused again, then Reed laid down his equipment and started around the table to throw him out manually. That's when the guy finally left. Afterwards, I know Dr. Reed felt ashamed that he'd let someone get under his skin to that level, but nobody blamed him.*
>
> *~ Elaine Russell, RN*

By 1970, I was ready for a new challenge. Dr. Delp, who was Chair of Medicine at KU, very much wanted me to stay, but I recognized the limitations in the university setting. I wanted a separate section of the hospital dedicated to heart surgery. In a limited way, KU complied. They made me a full professor, and guaranteed seven beds, but there were things I wanted to accomplish that weren't going to happen at KUMC. I recognized the need for an entire cardio-thoracic program, but the university wasn't ready to commit to anything on that scale. So I resigned from KU and set my sights on another major hospital in Kansas City: St. Luke's. I wanted to build a state of the art heart center that could meet the demands of the future because, without a doubt, that future was already happening for heart patients.

Robert Wagstaff, chairman of the St. Luke's board, was enthusiastic about the opportunity. The hospital lacked equipment and an experienced heart surgeon, but Saint Luke's was ready to commit to establishing a heart program there with my leadership. I was being recruited pretty heavily, and there was considerable professional jealousy over the idea that a red carpet was being rolled out for me by the top brass at St. Luke's. I resigned from KU in November and applied for permission to operate at St. Luke's. I received medical privileges there in early December 1970. However, the administrative support didn't ensure a unanimous back-slapping welcome for me. In fact, I learned that some of the St. Luke's doctors were aggressively campaigning against my arrival. By a vote taken at their annual staff meeting, my privileges were rescinded.

It was Christmas time, and Mary sat down on the stairs and cried as she overheard the conversation between two cardiologists from St. Luke's who came over to give me the news. I didn't have a job. I was in a precarious situation . . . unemployed with a wife and three little boys at home. Sitting in my garage was a $25,000 heart-lung machine I purchased with my own money to take to St. Luke's where, the fellows told me solemnly, I no longer had privileges. "It was such a low point," Mary recalled. "We had little kids, no Christmas. To think that they would do that to him was just devastating." It was a low point in my career. I thought I was going to have to start doing insurance physicals for a living. I had no office space at St. Luke's since I had no privileges there. Those were confusing, anxiety-ridden days. Thankfully, my privileges were restored after the politics got worked out at St. Luke's.

A friend of ours invited me to set up my practice in his medical office space, but then reneged on the offer when it was met with resistance from his partner—more political fallout. Then Dr. Wally McKee saved the day. Wally was an internist at St. Luke's who also happened to be my neighbor. I was glad to be able to use his examining rooms and had a desk in the hallway in his offices. I paid him rent, and I was on call 24/7/365—every single day and night without a break for a year. It was a bit harried to say the least. Making the transition from KU to St. Luke's was anything but smooth, but I hung in there. Without Suchint Wathanacharoen, I couldn't have done it.

Dr. Suchint Wathanacharoen or "Such" (pronounced Sooch) came to America from Thailand, and completed his training at KU in 1968. He came with me as an assistant, and stayed until he retired in 2009. Additionally, Dr. Ivan Crosby, who was from Australia, was in the middle of his residency in thoracic surgery at KU under my leadership, joined us at St. Luke's to complete his training there.

I didn't know if I could make a go of it on my own, but with their help and thanks to the support of cardiologists Dr. James Crockett, Dr. Ben McAllister, and Dr. Tim King, things were looking up within a few months. In 1971, I started MidAmerica Thoracic & Cardiovascular Surgeons, Inc., (MATCS) a private practice group with privileges at St. Luke's Hospital and set my sights on getting the best and brightest to work with me.

$\mathcal{A}$nn Goad was critically important in supporting our newly developing cardiac surgery program. As St. Luke's OR Supervisor, Ann greased the wheels when she could have just held the line on the Surgical Administration Committee's (SAC) status quo. Fortunately, she wasn't intimidated by the pressure from the other surgeons who were competing for time and space. She arranged the OR scheduling so we could do the maximum cases efficiently, and she saw to it that we were staffed with the best people. Her support made it possible for us to be successful, and our success gave us the credibility our heart program required to win over the naysayers. I'll be forever indebted to Ann.

After one year, Dr. Arnold Killen joined us from Vanderbilt University. Arnold was a very dedicated, capable, experienced cardiac surgeon. Much of the success and quality of our program was due to his contributions. As the program continued to grow, we needed more help. We invited Dr. Bill Hamaker to join us in 1987, and subsequently added Dr. Jeffrey Piehler, Dr. Michael Borkon, Dr. Michael Gorton, and Dr. Greg Muehlebach over the course of the next several years.

> *I was a surgeon in the army during Viet Nam and I was a marathon runner. St. Luke's was up to its eyeballs in alligators and since I'd earned my bones, so to speak, and was ready to get straight to work, I fit the bill. Bill Reed offered me the job the same day I interviewed. Later on, he said my background convinced him I had the stamina for their OR.*
>
> ~ *Bill Hamaker, MD*

> *My senior partners had great confidence in Bill, so they founded a practice at St. Luke's to assure that they would have a great surgeon to operate on their patients. Reed was just a gifted surgeon . . . he's just got it. When he went to St. Luke's, Hugh Bell and Lynn Kindred followed because they knew that it would work anywhere Bill Reed was. His presence guaranteed success.*
>
> ~ *Charles Porter, MD*

From 1971 to 1988, I was Director of Thoracic Surgery at St. Luke's. We were going like gangbusters. I was operating five days a week—the first surgeon to go forty straight cases without a mortality. We still had a long way to go, but in the first year of practice at St. Luke's, I did 250 heart operations; the following year I did 400. With Arnold Killen on board we took it higher. I was doing 500 myself, and we totaled almost 700 as a whole department in a year—an unprecedented number for the hospital. I performed the first heart transplant at St. Luke's in 1985. All the kids came to me—I was doing congenital as well as adult surgery. There were times in my practice when I'd go 100 surgeries in a row without a single death.

> *His survival rate was bar none. We did a thousand pump-cases in 1981. In those days, he was the best in the city.*
>
> *~ Elaine Russell, RN*

> *He's the best heart surgeon I've ever seen. I used to go in the OR and watch him. His big hands were moving so fast and his patients seemed to do better. It had to do with the speed he worked with, how he made sure he didn't get into trouble. It was impressive to watch the way he worked.*
>
> *~ Lynn Kindred, MD, Cardiologist*

> *Bill planned to become a psychiatrist, but he got into cardiovascular surgery instead and realized he had uncommon talents. He really loved taking care of people's hearts, but he always knew which patients might be going to have some emotional problems after their surgery. Sometimes he'd call me and say I think I'm going to need you to do a consultation on a patient I'm taking to surgery. He would always be right. I'd get a call from the nurses a day or two later, and the patient he'd mentioned would often be suffering severe depression already. Bill is the only surgeon I've ever worked with who had that kind of sensitivity.*
>
> *~ Jo Jeanne Callaway, MD, Psychiatrist*

Mostly because I was a family man or constantly on call, I'd pass on the invites to let loose on a Saturday night, but having fun outside of work was important. When my schedule on all fronts cleared so I could let down long enough to do some "team-building" with my colleagues, we'd go out. I'm not sure of the details of one particular evening—except I vowed it would be the last of this particular kind. I do remember whimpering as I lay on the tile floor beside the toilet in my bathroom beseeching, "Liver, do your work." Believe me, after the party's over and it's time to call it a day, doctors are just people, too.

If we did blow off some steam once in a while, I think it was justified given the intensity of the work we were doing. The hardest part of it was losing a patient. It didn't happen to me very often, but every surgeon loses some patients. Having to go and tell the family was the worst part of my practice. Once after losing a man on the table, I went out to tell his wife he didn't make it and she ran up and down the halls screaming, "You killed my husband!" Another time, I went out and informed the patient's spouse that her husband was going to be ok. She looked almost disappointed and replied, "Well, now what am I going to do?" People's reactions never ceased to amaze me. I learned to be prepared for anything—to keep my emotions in check.

The prevailing thought on this seems to be that surgeons see too much death to experience it personally . . . that they become necessarily detached so it doesn't affect them too deeply. Personally, I never could relate to that perspective. Certainly, I would put on my game face and go relate the bad news, but inside I was suffering. I'll never forget the wife of a man we lost in the OR who listened patiently as I explained all the things we had tried. She said, "Dr. Reed, I imagine you must be feeling as bad as me. I know you did everything you could, and I thank you for trying so hard. Thank you for doing everything you did to try and save my husband." I think I might have been as emotional as she was in that moment, and struggled to maintain my reserve. That's what patients and their families need from their surgeon—a Rock of Gibraltar even when the ground is shaking beneath his or her feet.

Looking Back

It didn't go well yesterday
even though I tried
It left an empty place
How do I fill it?
Gone from the lives
of loved ones
a picture now incomplete
How do we return another day
to the site of so much sorrow?
How do we replace yesterday
with a new tomorrow?
As well as we can
reach out with love
and join together
whether holding on or
letting go . . . there will be joy
on any day where
our lives touch

~ William Reed

There's no way to explain the aloneness surgeons experience when they're in those cases that become more and more complicated. A patient in for a valve procedure and repeat bypass . . . uncovering more and more scar tissue that requires total concentration for five hours; millimeter by millimeter. You have to get through that scar tissue and find those arteries. They're not bright red and bright blue like in the textbooks— you have to go find them.

~ Charles Porter, MD

I'll never forget Michael McCloskey's case, he was right on the cusp of his adult life but we knew he wasn't going to make it without a transplant. When I got the call that a donor heart was ready, I had only just arrived in Colorado for a ski vacation with my family. I had to rent another car and get back to the airport fast. Unbelievably, I had to change a flat tire on the way down the mountains. I hired a private pilot who flew me back to Kansas City. It was a high drama, but at least he had a happy ending. Michael went on to become a successful engineer with a wonderful family of his own.

The years at St. Luke's ushered in a new era for cardiac care. As Program Director for Thoracic Surgery, I established the residency for heart surgery at St. Luke's—an important accomplishment for a small, non-university hospital. Next, Ben McAllister and I developed a vision for a center that would focus on patients with cardiac disease. It came out of a conversation we had over dinner, ideas doodled on napkins, the sort of thing that happens when you are talking with someone who shares your dream. Ben and I had the same idea of how cardiac care should be.

I was twenty-four years old and had just graduated from Kansas State University with a degree in Engineering when I started feeling sick and then sicker. The diagnosis was dilated cardiomyopathy, which meant my heart was too weak to pump blood. To be honest, I was in shock. I didn't realize anything was seriously wrong with me and then I was being confronted with news that I was near death. The enormity of the situation was hard for me to grasp at that age. It became clear I would need a transplant, so I was placed on the waiting list.

Eventually, my heartbeat became seriously unstable so I was hospitalized at St. Luke's. They tried a medicine that had just been approved by the FDA to stabilize my heart rhythm. It worked so I got to go home with my parents. When we got the call that a donor heart was available, we got right into the car in Wichita and drove to Kansas City. It was two in the morning on April 30, 1987, when we arrived. I was the eleventh person to receive a heart transplant at St. Luke's. I don't remember much about the surgery itself, of course, only waking up with tubes and all these ventilators and bells, the feeling of being in a fog. I was in a lot of pain, but somehow also feeling better. My heart was functioning. A lot of things got better right away. I remember Dr. Reed checking on me. I remember his calmness . . . how he brought a sense of calm. He instilled confidence in me that it was going to be ok. I knew I was in good hands.

His life work gave me back my life. I celebrated my twenty-fifth birthday in the hospital during recovery."

~ Michael McCloskey, heart transplant patient

We knew it was critical to have all of our heart patients in the same place so the doctors, nurses and all the specialized equipment would be quickly accessible. There were times when a patient coded and I was literally pumping on his chest between the ICU on one floor and the OR on another. We'd be pushing that gurney towards an elevator that might be out of service, so we'd have to transport the patient through the main hallway to use the public elevator. The patient's family and perfect strangers were watching the whole thing happen. The physical setting was a challenge, to put it mildly. A complete redesign was urgently needed. In the early 1970s, there weren't many cardiovascular equipment companies yet, so it took some convincing. A heart hospital with a singular focus—it was a novel idea.

> Bill told me that at one point he went to the St. Luke's administrators to get more equipment and was told, "If you want more ventilators then buy them yourself." One administrator actually suggested that Bill take his patients to another hospital—that's what he was fighting. But Bill and Ben sold it to the board. Once they got the momentum with that, they just kept going.
>
> ~ Charles Porter, MD

There was a lot of resistance to the idea that cardiology should be given special attention. Competition for funds and human resources was stiff, and professional jealousy was vast. Changing the way a hospital functions is never easy, but the value of a heart hospital would prove impossible to ignore.

Early on, the cardiac care program at St. Luke's generated profit for the hospital. It was clear that the program deserved to be a priority. We needed more "beds" which are a kind of currency in every hospital. Getting them was a long, drawn-out process following a rigid state protocol. Charles Kimball, CEO of Midwest Research Institute, was tremendously influential in helping us make that happen. Ultimately, we received permission to go ahead with construction after more than five years spent in the state-required process. It was an agonizingly slow ordeal. I remember an open meeting before the Missouri Health Planning Authority that extended until 1:30am when it was apparent that we might not get approval. Finally, it was my turn to address the group. I testified that I couldn't believe it could be so hard to just do the right thing for patients. Mary and I returned home from that hearing at two in the morning, utterly exhausted.

Finally, a scaled-down version of our proposal was approved and in 1980, the Mid America Heart Institute was dedicated. It was one of the first hospitals in America exclusively devoted to cardiac care. The pay-off was immediate. Subsequently, St. Luke's expanded our program with three more floors and a helipad to meet the demand for these services. That demand kept growing and so did the Mid America Heart Institute. Over the course of nearly two decades that followed, I was fortunate to be involved in the design, development, and implementation of an unprecedented standard of cardiac care that saved thousands of lives. After the excruciating losses in the early years, I watched with gratitude and awe as survival became the norm.

It was 1999. I was on vacation with my sons fishing the Green River in Utah. Under the wide horizon of the western sky, only the sound of moving water and the occasional hoot or holler when somebody landed a nice trout interrupted the tranquility around me. In general, my life felt equally calm. I had done what I set out to do both personally and professionally. I was seventy-two years old, an age when most of my peers had already retired to their golf carts. I knew I wasn't ready for that, but nor was I prepared for what happened next. Maybe a dark cloud moved over the sun or a crow circled above me . . . maybe the trees tried to tell me. I didn't notice anything foreboding. I was watching the eddies, fly-casting, and listening to the leaves whispering in the cottonwoods. "Peace like a river" stayed with me right up to the moment we returned to the cabin that evening to find an urgent message for me to call MATCS—my office. Something bad was going down.

To understand the import of what happened next, it's important to understand how the dynamics at St. Luke's worked. There were two cardiology groups in private practice that served the hospital's heart patients: Cardiovascular Consultants (CC), and Mid-America Cardiology (MAC). Both private practice groups referred their surgical cases to MidAmerica Thoracic & Cardiovascular Surgeons, or MATCS, which was my group. At that time, MATCS did all the cardiac-thoracic surgery for St. Luke's.

Bending my ear into a radio phone in the Utah wilderness, I tried to make sense of what my medical partner was telling me. Over the past year there had been a series of secret meetings between St. Luke's hospital administration and Cardiovascular Consultants . . . today there was an announcement. St. Luke's was planning to give CC exclusive control over the hospital's cardiovascular program. All of this happened behind closed doors without any involvement or consideration of MAC or MATCS. The result was a sweet deal for CC who would gain all the control and competitive advantages at St. Luke's.

As we learned more, it became abundantly clear that the proposed plan would likely mean the end of MAC as we knew it, a group we'd collaborated with successfully for thirty years. Further, I couldn't see how this was going to benefit the overall heart program; in fact, I thought it would significantly limit our future growth. Then there was the unprofessionalism of the process—all the covert actions and disregard of all the vested parties—mildly put, that broke my sense of trust with St. Luke's hospital administration.

I'd only been president of MAC a few months before St. Luke's announced their agreement with Cardiology Consultants. The process of negotiating that agreement had been carried out confidentially to the exclusion of my group and Bill's surgical group, MATCS. Kansas City's medical community isn't all that big, so MAC had to take stock. We sat down and made a decision to stick together to maintain our independent identity. We decided not be folded into the St. Luke's plan, which was on the table but not appealing to MAC. We had a strong agenda when it came to our standards for patient care, medical education and research. Early on, I had talked to Bill Reed. In fact, I remember calling him from the doctor's lounge at St. Luke's on a deserted weekend. I wasn't real sure how he would react to the announcement of the covert management agreement, but almost immediately Bill and most of his partners recognized that they didn't want to be a part of that arrangement. They were interested in potentially doing something with MAC, whatever that meant.

KU's cardiology program had hit hard times by end of '90s, so I'd called the Dean to ask if there was any interest in discussing collaboration that might be in both our best interests. Dean Debbie Powell said yes, but she didn't have any money. We'd have to appeal to Irene Cummings who was then CEO for KUMC. The whole process of negotiation took about a year and a half. Bill was the principal for the surgeons; I was principal for the cardiologists. We hired our own legal representation and negotiated different contracts, but it was all done together. Surgeon issues are a little different than those of a cardiology group, but we collaborated closely through the entire process.

I gained a whole lot of respect for Bill's keen sense of strategic thinking and ability to negotiate for things that are important. For example, one of the things Bill really pushed for was a commitment in our contract that the hospital would begin work on a new facility within three years of our arrival. I didn't really appreciate that this was all that important. I figured if we had the right people with the right intention, we could do this anywhere. But boy, when a hospital commits tens of millions of dollars and announces it publicly, that tells the community about its importance. And in fact, having a new facility designed for cardiology exclusively does make a difference in the quality we could deliver. Bill's foresight proved a huge advantage to the standards we achieved at KUMC's Heart Institute.

~ Steve Owens, MD, Cardiologist and former president, Mid-America Cardiology Group

Making a covert deal was an underhanded thing for St. Luke's to do. When the guys in cardiology asked me to get involved, I realized I already was involved—no avoiding it. Although the implications to MATCS weren't dire, the situation called for action. So the next question was what kind of involvement I wanted to have, and the answer to that was to do the right thing—morally and ethically. I just couldn't condone the way this had gone down; going on with business as usual felt like a kind of tacit approval. After a lot of deliberation, I knew I was prepared to leave St. Luke's over this. As soon as that word got around, there were quite a few people that followed suit.

It was a big move to leave KU for the first time and establish a heart center at St. Luke's. That was a huge step, but he would take an even bigger one when he left St. Luke's and came back to KUMC.

~ Irene Thompson (formerly Irene Cumming President and CEO, University of Kansas Medical Center), University Health Consortium President

The transition from St. Luke's to KUMC was awkward if not acutely painful at times. The administration of St. Luke's might have been counting on my early retirement and a selective poaching of MAC talent after it announced the new regime, but in actuality, nothing could have been further from the truth. Once it learned that MATCS and MAC were in negotiations to move their groups to KUMC, the top brass at St. Luke's was not pleased. "Registered letters were sent to all our homes, sort of a 'don't do this, you'll be sorry, you're going to want to come back' tactic. St. Luke's attempted to make things difficult for some of our members by requiring their re-credentialing . . . that sort of thing. It took months to make the transition . . . very awkward," Owens recalled.

It was a stressful time, but everyone faces such crises at some point in life. The choices you make in those moments set the stage for the next things that are possible. There I was in the centrifuge of all that drama when I was hit by another blow: I was diagnosed with prostate cancer. Bowing out of things at that point was unthinkable. So I had cancer surgery in that fall, and then got back to work as quickly as possible. My attitude as a person suffering from cancer was that I wanted to practice medicine as long as I could do it competently, but then St. Luke's called that into question.

I had to jump through a number of hoops including having a physical evaluation before I could continue practicing medicine at St. Luke's. Fortunately, I passed the physical with flying colors. Every day I would just try to do the next right thing, and eventually, I got through it. I continued to move forward because there were a lot of people depending on me to lead the charge. We had to make the transition to KU work, and to establish the cardiac care center at KU successfully.

We were all shocked at the way St. Luke's handled the situation— like picking one child over another with favoritism. Most of us didn't want any part of that. St. Luke's administration was pretty underhanded about it. They tried to discredit Dr. Reed and make the case that he couldn't operate based on his age

*and health. The feeling was definitely strong that sticking with
Dr. Reed was the way to go, but there were repercussions for
those of us who left. It was an awful time to be at St. Luke's . . .
watching the treatment administration was dishing out.*

~ *Elaine Russell, RN*

Throughout the painful process, Steve Owens and I remained
steadfast that there would be no public acrimony over St. Luke's
decisions. Steve recalled, "Even though there were hard feelings, it
didn't spill over in a public arena. St. Luke's is a fine hospital. We
have respect for the work they do, and we all have friends there. For
doctors to throw rocks at each other just generates anxiety in the
minds of patients. It makes us all look bad."

We were both committed to doing what was best for patients. As
Steve said, "That's the north star, regardless of whose patients they
are. Bill held the high ground in spite of being vilified by some of his
colleagues at St. Luke's. He never moaned and groaned about it, he
just kept on doing the right thing."

Although we had been professional partners and close family
friends, the St. Luke's controversy found Ben McAllister and I on
different sides of the issue. Ben was with Cardiology Consultants,
and he tried to sell me on the new deal, but I thought it was
unconscionable. He told me I was making the biggest mistake of my
life . . . that if I didn't go along with it, I'd be throwing away my
career and legacy. I hoped he was wrong, because this wasn't about
my legacy, it was about doing the right thing.

The turn into the new millennium was a time of profound change.
I was on point to make the transition from St. Luke's to KUMC. I
felt the weight of everyone's expectations. Many individuals in both
the surgical and cardiology groups came on board because, as Bill
Hamaker put it, "I knew if Bill Reed was involved that it would be
successful." I was keenly aware of the professionals whose careers
hinged on making the move successfully, Dr. Gorton and Dr. Piehler

both chose to transition to KU with me at that time. We all felt a responsibility to the patients who opted to make the switch along with us as well.

We were all very excited about the possibilities for Reed and his team coming over to KU, but it was a challenging negotiation. There were variables and unique requirements for the surgeons, the cardiologists, all of the staff, really, as well as the physical environment, and mostly for the patients themselves, although those were really positive considerations. We spent a year in dialogue about what our partnership would look like, and that conversation included twenty-three cardiologists. Everyone had a voice, but Reed was the lead. At one point, I think we figured everything out to our satisfaction, at least theoretically, so I went on a much-needed vacation to the Bahamas.

I'd hardly arrived when I got a call from Reed that his doctors had some issues with the contract language. Things could have gone terribly wrong at that point, but everybody had their hearts in the right place and we wanted to get it right. So Bill parked himself on the phone and so did I, although for me that meant sitting in a tiny, non-air conditioned room about the size of a phone booth for the better part of a day and half while we ironed everything out. Bill Reed was the consummate professional throughout that agonizing process. His diligence in taking care of his people while collaborating with us was the key to pulling this off. I just can't say enough good things about that man."

~ Irene Thompson (formerly Irene Cumming, President and CEO, KUMC), University Health Consortium President

William Reed testifies at a legislative hearing.

CHAPTER 7

Visionary

Bill is humble and patient, brilliant and visionary. He has convictions that stem from his knowledge—he knows what he knows, and why. I think his greatness is because he's such a good thinker. He becomes an expert far beyond what the normal person would bother to learn in whatever he puts his mind to. He is willing to keep pursuing things that will advance heart care, patient care, the institution. He can see the needs in various arenas. He's passionate about his vision, and his vision is always right.

~ Betty Keim, formerly with
the Kansas Hospital Authority Board

Life has taught me that you never want to run away from something, only move towards something that's better. When I decided to leave St. Luke's and return to KU, it was initially prompted by what was going down back there, but, ultimately, my motivation was to make something really good out of a bad situation. I never thought of the move as a retreat, but rather, as an advance towards a vision I wanted to make real. I was excited for the opportunity to come "home" to the place I started from almost forty-five years earlier as a new member of the house staff in 1954. So my surgical group joined ranks with Mid-America Cardiology and we returned to KU.

Everyone had such great respect. There was a feeling like, "Dr. Reed is coming home again!" I remember St. Luke's tried to embarrass Reed and take away his dignity, but he stayed above it all, and never responded to the attacks. It was a big move to leave KU the first time to start a heart center at St. Luke's, and an even bigger step to leave St. Luke's and come back. He had a vision, and he was going to make it happen. He knows how to push, but does so for the right reasons so people don't feel manipulated.

~ Irene Thompson (formerly Irene Cumming, President and
CEO, KUMC), University Health Consortium President

In the late 1990s, the University of Kansas Medical Center was not perceived as a respected healthcare institution. The reputation in the community was that this wasn't the place to be if you were sick. Even a survey of its own staff showed low levels of confidence. The Kansas Legislature established the Kansas Hospital Authority in 1998 when KUMC had just eighteen days of operating income to work with and a national consultant's advice to close the place down or make it a charity hospital. Many friends and colleagues pointed out that my retirement would be entirely justified rather than walk into the fray at KUMC following my highly successful run at St. Luke's. I was over seventy and recuperating from prostate cancer—not the ideal age or state of mind for a man facing the biggest career challenge of his life.

He's a courageous man. He had the courage to come back to KU—a place that was frankly struggling, and "struggling" doesn't begin to describe it. We had no heart program at all. Reed put his entire reputation on the line. He chose to come here when he could have gone anywhere, or even stayed at St. Luke's, but he came "home."

~ Bob Page, President and CEO
The University of Kansas Hospital

Night Shades

Across the top of the woods
I see the night descending on
the tallest tree
Bereft now of leaves
and life once
giant of this
forest now waiting
to return to the earth
with a wind or the winter
People are a lot like trees
Some spreading dominant
across the Sky
Briefly – too briefly
Feeling the freedom and
Breeze on their faces
Never anticipating
the return to
their beginning

~ William Reed

In spite of it all, when we signed the contract in November 2000, and I walked back through the doors of my old and new home: the University of Kansas Medical Center. I felt invigorated by the challenge. It's a good feeling to be part of starting something up. Once we got to KU, there was a lot of work to be done in terms of clinical quality and patient service. I think to Irene's credit, they really did listen carefully and respond constructively to the concerns and suggestions we made. I think some of that was because we had the credibility.

Dr. Reed certainly could have moved around, I think Mayo's recruited him intensely. But he refused to go different places because he was committed to making the thing he was doing successful, and you can't keep doing that by moving around a lot. He got the best people and it shows. His focus wasn't on compensation or ego, it was on building a program. I think if you look at the history of cardiac care here, when we started, we were counteracting a lot of negative trends in the industry and at KU in particular. He came here and set up something that worked. The thing I like about him is there's just no pretense. He is who he is; he is not going to tell you one thing and somebody else another thing. Dr. Reed is straightforward, trustworthy, and he cares about everybody. He treats everybody equally—the people who clean his office get treated just like he treats the CEO. He doesn't treat people different based on rank. If anybody could have turned things around at KU, it was Bill Reed.

~ Jeffrey Kramer, MD, Cardiothoracic Surgeon

To make this start-up successful, I knew we had to have buy-in from everyone involved, and by everyone I meant everyone. The first large organizational meeting we had was with the nursing and support staff in the nursing auditorium. There were four of us surgeons who spoke to about one hundred there. Our primary message was, "If you are concerned about your patient's progress, call us 24/7. That's the way it works now." I have never regretted going in to see a patient that the nurse was concerned about; almost without exception, nurses are right in their assessment. That was one of the values we were bringing to this new venture.

Decades of my own experience have solidified my views on this: nurses are not just an extension of the doctor. They are immeasurably important in their own right with their own unique skills and life-saving service. Certainly, Mary's professional background has increased my awareness of the issues that nurses face. Too many times I've heard, "Oh, I'm just the nurse," when discussing a patient's status. I gently assert, "You are not 'just a nurse' . . . you are a nurse, and your opinion here is critical to this discussion and to the work we're doing together."

At KU, Bill Reed created the bow-wave—that's the wake that precedes the bow of a boat moving through the water. It marked the course for KU Hospital's cardiovascular success in the 21st Century. There is no academic hospital in the country that transformed from beached whale to Olympic star in a period of ten years. That's the success that Bill's leadership and vision created at KU Hospital.

~ Charles Porter, MD

In the fall of 2000, KU had three cardiologists and no heart surgeons, so for practical purposes, we were building from the ground up. I wanted everyone invested in our success, so we continued to meet with nurses, orderlies—anybody who touched a patient had a valuable role and input to give us. I set up committees to discuss how we would do this—what we would build together. Within just a couple years, things were turning around and headed in the right direction for KUMC. I was seventy-five years old when I stepped away from the operating table and the full transition to the next generation of surgeons was made.

> *There was just so much professional respect from his cardiologists. They had faith in him, everybody did. He cared as much about the housekeeper as the lead surgeon. They were all equivalent in terms of achieving the desired outcome. And Dr. Reed delivered great outcomes. Everybody wanted their patients served by the best cardiovascular team, and he was leading it. He had the credibility with staff and patients. Everybody trusted his judgment.*
>
> ~ *Irene Thompson (formerly Irene Cumming, President and CEO, KUMC), University Health Consortium President*

Although I retired from the operating room, I continued to see patients. I was appointed Chair of the Department of Cardiovascular Diseases, and within that department I also chaired the quality assurance committee and medical morbidity and mortality conference. Plans for the building of our heart hospital were underway, and throughout all of it, I felt the same passion for the work that fueled me for over sixty years. The University of Kansas Medical Center now features the largest heart program in this part of the country. Today it's an excellent hospital, ranked number two in America as an academic medical center (by the University Health System Consortium's Quality and Accountability Study, Fall 2012). Patients have wonderful experiences here.

> *Actually, he built two programs from the ground up—the first at St. Luke's and next the one at KUMC—and both have been the greatest success of their era.*
>
> ~ *Jeffrey Kramer, MD*

STARMAGA

Heart
AND soul

He was there at KC's
first open-heart surgery.
He performed the first
heart transplant here.
And now that William Reed
is retired from surgery?
He's still trailblazing.

BY MICHAEL HUMPHREY
PHOTOS BY TAMMY LJUNGBLAD

Cover of Kansas City STAR Magazine, January 8, 2000

CHAPTER 8

Mentor

I always looked for people smarter than me to find out what their opinions were. As a learning strategy, it's a good one. As a teaching tool, it's incumbent upon us to share what we know . . . generously.

~ William Reed

Both of my hands were inside the patient's chest cavity. With one hand, I was making an incision in the left atrial appendage while the fingers of my other hand squeezed the valve open through which I would insert a dilator. It would have been a good time to have a third hand, especially since the thing I hoped wouldn't happen did happen—the heart fibrillated. It wasn't beating. Not good. The circumstances were now dire. A closed mitral valvotomy was still a risky surgery in 1960, and this was only the first or second operation I'd done as a new member of the KU medical staff—no one was calling me Dr. Cool yet. I needed my third hand, fast. As calmly as I could, I asked if someone would call Dr. Kittle for an assist while I carefully pulled the instrument out of the left ventricle. My mentor swiftly sent this reply: It's time to grow up, kid.

Every mentor senses the right moment to cut the cord completely—hoping everything leading up to it created the best chance for success. In that moment, I didn't feel ready even if Fred

Kittle did. In retrospect, I was, and the operation was successful. I dilated the valve, took my finger out of the atrium, stopped the bleeding, defibrillated the heart with electrical pads, and we were in good shape. The heart was repaired, the patient recovered, and I, the surgeon, learned something very important about myself by myself. That's the kind of confidence that comes to an individual when diligent preparation joins effective action. Good mentoring sets up that possibility, and self-assurance is the gain.

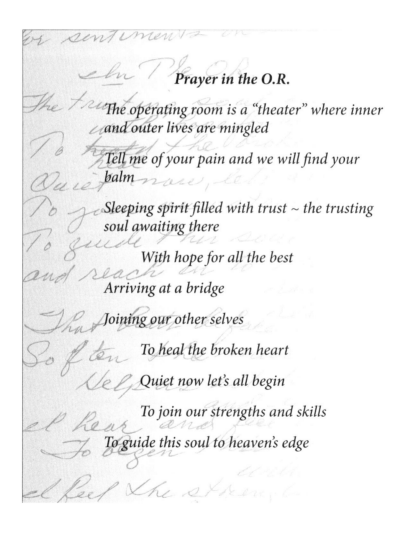

Prayer in the O.R.

*The operating room is a "theater" where inner
and outer lives are mingled*

*Tell me of your pain and we will find your
balm*

*Sleeping spirit filled with trust ~ the trusting
soul awaiting there*

With hope for all the best

Arriving at a bridge

Joining our other selves

To heal the broken heart

Quiet now let's all begin

To join our strengths and skills

To guide this soul to heaven's edge

And reach into the rhythmic reality

That beats before us

bring that soft music back again

Fix the broken part

All to teach and listen

I hear and feel we're ready

To begin this dance

With the Gods

I feel the strength and

Confidence of us together

We're all in tune

We are with you - Hold to us.

The machine hums the vital functions

The fluids again nourish and the

Great Spirit flourishes

For this soul and for all who

lulled you back to life

we sing together Amen

~ William Reed

The mentors who shared their wisdom and guidance with me are long gone now, but much of what they imparted is as true today as it was when I started my career . . . and it will be true long after I'm gone. Even with all our medical advances and new technologies, certain foundations aren't altered by circumstances, personality or the season of life in which they occur. They can't be learned from a book or replaced by technology. These are the things we experience directly—when theory becomes practice. Not just the knowledge but the wisdom . . . the validation of it all from someone who has navigated the dark stretches and made it out on the other side. I have a strong sense of duty when it comes to mentoring, particularly young women and men who are choosing a career in medicine. This is as good a time and place as any to share what I have to say to you.

Being a physician is the most unique calling one can receive. That's how I've always felt about this work. It offers the opportunity to:

- Discover the miracles within us . . . to see how our bodies work.

- Learn and grow with ever-expanding knowledge about human disease and treatment.

- Hold the sacred responsibility of another human's life in your hands.

- Sustain the energy, commitment and love of someone's family circle.

- Feel a sense of purpose and priority that never diminishes.

As such, being a physician requires a kind of commitment and tenacity that not everyone possesses. I have been famously intolerant of people not doing their best, even if I never was prone to histrionics. I was tough, in terms of expectations, but my team knew that any disapproval from me wasn't to belittle them, but because I recognized they could do better. In the early days of cardiac care, teaching what I was doing while I was doing it, or even while I was inventing it at times, was the only way many would learn this field. The stakes were so high that I simply had to get the best out of everybody in the OR. You can be a hard-assed teacher and students will come away respecting you for it. It serves the purpose of helping them achieve their best potential. That, combined with being there for the right reasons on a personal level, is how lives are saved.

To the student who wants to be a doctor, I want you to consider these things:

- Do it for yourself, not for someone else or to fulfill somebody else's expectations for you.

- Find a mentor who is a physician and explore his or her experience and ideas.

- Don't limit yourself out of fear of the demands ahead of you.

- Develop your ability to take in what others are trying to tell you; the best doctors who are most loved by their patients are good listeners.

- Recognize that the patient usually tells you what is wrong with him or her (if you listen).

- Run an inventory of your own attributes; can you commit to the hard work, long hours, level of responsibility, strain on your family and personal life?

- Weigh the positives against the negatives including . . .
  - Financials
  - Motivations
  - Lifestyle considerations
  - Family support
  - Fear of failure
  - Doubts about who you are

- Ask yourself if this is your calling; expect an answer.

If you believe you have the call, spend as much time as you can with someone who is in active clinical practice. One doesn't really appreciate the emotion and challenge of medicine until one gets into the clinical years. Discuss your goals and concerns with a clinical mentor you can respect. Get close to him or her. If you're the physician who needs to mentor that medical student or young doctor, then give yourself to that. Share the good and not so good experiences together, and how you both feel about them.

> *He's been a great partner. This program has been recognized for a long time now, and that is a reflection of his commitment, of his professionalism in dealing with folks who may not be quite as professional. He's a tremendous role model. When we review cases where another doctor's behavior is an issue, he is often asked to step in and talk to the doc. A few words from him carry a lot more weight than a reprimand from a superior. He's never been unwilling to do that.*
>
> *~ Lynn Kindred, MD*

Remember, as a physician you see people at a vulnerable time of their life . . . hundreds of thousands of people who might otherwise be strong and capable but have been brought low by sickness or disease. They're coming to you saying, "Here I am, do what you will," and that's where you have to have that intrinsic feeling of truly wanting to help them. I don't think you can fabricate that emotion. You've just got to want to help make somebody better.

Life changes our perception and receptivity. With experience and exposure, you become more aware of the hurts in other people, which can make you either more receptive or more blocked if you haven't got the emotional maturity to be present with someone in pain. Patients will tell you what they're concerned about; their anxieties about death are heightened when facing cardiac surgery. Listen to what they're saying to you and follow their lead. Generally, they're very open and receptive to meaningful discussion. A health crisis catapults you right into that space with them. Physicians need to prepare themselves for that moment—practice and role-play for it. It's important to find a mentor who can model good bedside behavior and emotional support. You should search your own feelings, attitude, and fortitude so you can be genuinely helpful at a time like that.

> *When I first came to work there, my ex-husband worked at St Luke's in the OR, and he had told me Dr. Reed was intimidating to people—up on this high pedestal. He didn't make them feel that way, they just did because he was so good. Dr. Reed was a wonderful boss to work for. He valued my opinion on things. I could talk to him about anything. In twenty years, I never saw him upset. He is a very even-keeled person . . . even in the OR. You'd hear stories about surgeons who went off, but never him. I told him that working for him was the best thing that happened to me when I moved here. He was so generous to me, but he's that way with everybody. People often sent him cards on the anniversary of their surgery. He always responded to them with a handwritten note of congratulations. He was great about that.*

> *~ Pat Kinsman, Reed's assistant from 1993 to 2013*

For the patient, your look can be worth more than your words. Meet him or her with a smile, sit down face to face, get personal. Right away, he or she will gain a sense of trust. I always believed that a physician must face his patients with optimism—that we were going to do together what needs to get done. You can frame something as frightening or encouraging, it's a conscious choice. So proactively develop a positive manner and vocabulary. Instead of speaking in terms of a two percent risk, you say ninety-eight times out of one hundred, you're going to walk out of here with your family . . . you'll be feeling better. It's been my experience that taking a hopeful position sets up the best outlook and communication with the patient and family.

One of my favorite stories exemplifies this. A cafeteria worker here at our hospital was delivering a dinner tray to a desperately sick woman. That patient was so overcome with anxiety that she couldn't swallow a bite and waved the tray away with, "What's the point, I'm going to die." But the cafeteria worker beamed a smile right back and replied, "Sister, we are not about dying here, we're about living . . . I am here to help you live." That's exactly the kind of attitude that gives comfort and builds confidence in patients. That kind of energy is contagious. It helps them get well.

One of the hardest things to teach young surgeons is when not to operate. The most dangerous surgeons are the ones who don't know their limitations. Experience taught me what I could and couldn't do for a patient. There was a point in my career when I learned that I shouldn't attempt certain things—like a patient with a really complicated congenital heart condition. I'd refer him or her to someone I thought might do a better job. I learned to be wary of stepping in after another surgeon had exhausted all the options and wanted my help with a patient who was showing fixed and dilated pupils. Nobody wants to give up, and I'd really have to search my soul for the right response. Unless I thought the benefit outweighed the risk, and that there would be some benefit, I wouldn't do it. Generally, the cardiologists would respect that. My approach was always to ask am I going to make this patient better? I'd be completely up front with the cardiologist if I thought I could get the patient through surgery, or else I'd admit it if I didn't think there'd be any or enough benefit to him or her.

Here's another truth: you're going to make mistakes. I know I have, in fact, I don't know any physician who hasn't. Learn from them. Someone who thinks failure is not a part of their make-up really doesn't understand and still has some hard lessons ahead of him or her. Many times, I thought everything had gone right, but then later I'd discover something was going wrong. If a patient was struggling, I'd get a call from the nurse to come back. I'd look for signs indicating there was a problem—the restlessness, the fingers "picking cotton" and the patient unable to get calm. If I had to stand by the bedside all night to take care of them, I would. We might have to go back into the OR where we'd find some internal bleeding or some other problem that needed immediate attention. Circumstances may be such that what you know you're capable of isn't possible or it won't work. No matter what you're doing, you have to be humble enough to realize you still have things to learn and that there are limitations. Arrogance in a cardiac surgeon can be deadly.

> *The finest moment I ever had with Bill was not as his partner, but when he came down to my son Ted's funeral in 2010. I was retired by then and only seeing Bill once or twice a year. I didn't know he was even aware of my son's passing, but he found out and drove 150 miles to the service. It meant a lot to me personally. I nearly broke down and cried when I saw him there. That's who he is. His sensitivity to others is amazing . . . how he goes the extra distance to be helpful.*
>
> *~ Bill Hamaker, MD*

Some doctors will do every procedure under the sun before giving up. That's not necessarily helpful or compassionate, from my point of view. As I see it, a surgeon's job includes recognizing that some heroic efforts are not going to improve the patient's life, however little of it remains. They may even result in more trauma. A patient's last days are better spent with family having experiences that help with acceptance and closure.

When the patient isn't going to make it, the tenor of your communication must be helpful and compassionate. Doctors cannot heal with their words, but having the right thing to say when there is no more hope can provide great consolation to the patient and family. In my experience, what most people want from their physician is a clear indication of when it's time to stop trying. Often the family is conflicted over the choices that need to be made at that point. As the physician, you have a responsibility to the patient and family in this process. I believe that role is to:

- Bring the hospital ethics specialists on board who can provide objective consultation as well as resources on hospice, palliative care, and end-of-life choices.

- Recap the medical perspective on the situation including what has been done and why it didn't work.

- Listen attentively to the patient's stated concerns and priorities; he or she will indicate what's important to discuss from their point of view.

- Restrain yourself from sharing your own religious beliefs; it's not appropriate to impose your personal theology on your patients and their family. Even if asked directly, you should tread lightly and be respectful of their values.

- Validate the family's diligence; you want them to feel resolved in their heart that they saw to it that everything that could be done was done, and that they did the right thing.

- Give them permission to let go; they are waiting to hear this verbally from an authority figure, and that is usually the physician, minister or, ideally, both.

There's so much in the news today on doctors cheating, over-charging, performing unnecessary operations, ordering non-essential tests, and whatever else constitutes bad news for the field of medicine. Whoever among us creates such bad press wasn't pursuing medicine for the right reasons, in my opinion. It is a great privilege for a human being to be in a position to help someone who is truly sick or in pain. We have to be able to do this in a compassionate way with the right skills and motivation. If that's not why you're going into medicine, then do something else.

I think Cormac McCarthy's *The Road* should be on the syllabus of required reading for anyone going into medicine. Are you carrying "the fire"? I hope that it takes hold of you—that you have both the passion as well as an innate sense of responsibility to do this work. This is a calling, but not everybody in medicine has it. If you're doing it because you want an affluent life with a wife flashing her diamond rings or your husband sailing his yacht, that's the wrong reason to be a doctor. That is not the fire.

There will be many hurdles to jump, but the biggest obstacle is usually your attitude. If a poor kid like me from the wrong side of town can become a heart surgeon, horseman and philanthropist, then what kind of excuse could anyone make for not overcoming the odds? I firmly believe that experiencing a disadvantaged childhood can provide powerful incentive and a host of survival skills. Among other things, it will teach you that . . .

1. One learns to play for survival; you will learn how to survive.

2. The scars heal, but you can still see and feel "the proud flesh."

3. You will discover who you are and your personal assets.

4. You learn how to accept being outscored but not defeated.

5. You learn not to think about defeat—it's not acceptable.

7. You learn that you can't do it alone.

8. You learn from failure what it takes to succeed.

9. You become more alert and sensitive to those in need around you.

10. You become more "wired" to pick up on cues that someone is in pain.

11. You won't be uncomfortable with people from lower socio-economic status.

12. You come to appreciate the joy of giving.

13. You have "been there" and can use your credibility to influence positive changes—sharing your own experience of poverty or deprivation is what makes the connection to others genuine.

14. It makes you stronger, more willing to give and love, more understanding, and a better mentor.

15. It all makes you a better person, and a better physician.

> *Bill Reed is sort of a Renaissance man. One minute he's talking about surgery, the next he's quoting poetry. He's very thoughtful, and interested in so many different things. He knows a lot about a lot of different things. I enjoy his company very much. He's been an important mentor to me. I've never had one negative interaction with him in twelve years . . . his honesty and integrity . . . so important. Sometimes I think "what would Bill do in this situation?" We talk politics, medical politics, the way of life in the US. He has remained active at the hospital, and we all see him as the elder statesman, or maybe a rock star.*
>
> *~ Jeffrey Kramer, MD*

Finally, when times are hard, remember why you wanted to be a doctor. As British Prime Minister Benjamin Disraeli said, "The secret of success is constancy of purpose." It's very easy to get lost between the greatest aspirations and smallest excruciating details of it all. It's easy to become exhausted and depleted, and difficult sometimes to remember why you came to this work. My advice is to find the thing that reminds you of who you are aside from a physician, nurse, or healthcare worker. Do that thing regularly. And if you're not born to be a doctor, don't become one. Find out what you are uniquely created to do on this earth and do that—whatever it is, that is also a calling.

Reaching Out

There is a need that lives within

our innermost Being

to recognize the hurt

around and among us.

Let us reach into

the throbbing pain and

apply ourselves as

balm . . . the healing touch

the best we can give

then keep only what we

gave away . . . and Hope

will make us all better

at joy and in our rejoicing

~ William Reed

William Reed at home, Stonecrest Farm

CHAPTER 9

Horseman

There's something about the outside of a horse

that's good for the inside of a man.

~ Winston Churchill

Doctoring will take every moment of time a physician can give it until the physician literally gives out. The key is not giving out. That means finding other things in life that fill you up instead of drain you. For me, time with my family was the reservoir of my replenishment. And for that reason, I was organizing a fishing trip to Christmas Island with my sons when my plans went awry.

I had always been healthy and health conscious—even my prostate cancer was detected early because I maintained a proactive wellness plan. So in 1984 when I had a routine EKG treadmill test in which a slight irregularity showed up, I put the vacation on hold. Upon further investigation, we learned that I had a high-grade "widow maker" that would require an immediate mammary bypass. In June, I went to a friend at the Cleveland Clinic in Ohio for the surgery so as not to put pressure on my own colleagues to do the operation.

For the next month, I recuperated then returned to work full-time. I was fifty-seven years old, fit and otherwise healthy, running daily and maintaining my regular work week of ten to twelve hours a day at the hospital. Each evening I was home for dinner with my family, but then I'd turn around and head back to the hospital if necessary. I was still doing heart transplant surgeries that could take all night. My schedule was grueling by anyone's standards. The close call with my heart was a reality check, and some changes were in order. I adjusted my diet and stopped taking night calls unless it was my own patient. The whole ordeal prompted me to take a hard look at my lifestyle. I knew I needed more balance in my life.

Although I wasn't ready to retire, I started to make a plan for something to do outside of medicine that would inspire and challenge me. The unhappiest people I know are those who have no life outside their work and then retire without a plan. Every human soul needs something worthwhile to do. Whatever that was for me, it had to make sense for the whole family. Mary and I discussed many options, but animals and pets of all kinds had always been a part of our lifestyle, so it was a natural thing to pursue something related to that as a passion.

Fishing and skiing vacations sustained me, but those were things the boys and I did that didn't fully include Mary. By late 1980s, my sons were older, married and pursuing their own interests. I wanted to find something we could all do together. My bookkeeper Betty was a member of the Kansas City Racing Stable, and she suggested I check out horses. The new Woodlands Racetrack was opening up in Kansas City, and I was intrigued. As a kid, Martin had always expressed interest in having a horse, and I had my own fond memories of the cart pony my dad kept around for a while. Mary's love for animals was legendary, and she had a special passion for horses in particular. Jeff and Bryan liked the idea, so everybody got behind this new venture that we could share as a family. That's how one of the greatest joys of my life began . . . raising and racing thoroughbreds.

I always wanted a horse. I loved horses. From age five to twelve, every birthday, Christmas, vacation, special event, I had to have a horse, so I have this huge horse collection at my parents' house that I'll give to my daughters one day. In 1990, the Woodlands Race Track opened up in Kansas City and Dad thought it would be nice to have a few ponies on that racetrack. Typical of my dad—he's quite competitive—he went straight to Keeneland Sales, which is a pretty exclusive horse auction in Kentucky. He got a couple horses that were too competitive to be racing at the Woodlands, so from the git-go, we were racing at Arlington Park in Chicago. Once we started winning consistently there, we went to Churchill Downs. Then there was Perfect Drift . . . he was like catching lightning in a bottle. Dad's horse farm has grown from "a couple ponies" at our local racetrack to this operation of thirty-five horses with a trainer, plus another trainer at Churchill Downs, and still another trainer that goes to Saratoga.

~ Martin Reed

This was a whole new branch of our life experience. At first, Mary was skeptical that competitive horseracing could possibly be good for the horse. Her answer to any horse concern was, "They should come home if they're limping!" That fit our hearts . . . we were all oriented in that direction. Our philosophy was that the horse came first. We weren't in it for the money or fame. We just wanted to have this exciting endeavor to share as a family—one that gave us an opportunity to be around these magnificent animals. We wanted to raise horses and race them in a way that showed our best stewardship of this responsibility. In return, the horses have taken care of us in ways we never imagined.

Soon enough it became abundantly clear that horses would be much more than a hobby for us—they became our way of life. I continued full-time medical practice, but started learning everything I could about raising thoroughbreds and horse racing. I met a trainer at the Woodlands Race Track in Kansas City who started showing

What a gift is horse to man.

Both of us love to eat and to look good.

We love to play games with each other.

We establish a pecking order for family and friends.

We see the doctor when we're sick.

We can disappoint and reject each other.

We thrive on competition and winning.

We can touch and nuzzle and heal one another.

We love our children and cry when they leave us . . .

we love each other through and through

. . . horses and men look out for each other.

~ William Reed

me the ropes. He suggested a trip to Keeneland Horse Auction in Kentucky so I could see a serious operation. We went and I bought two horses, KC Blues and Pleasure Return. I had a lot more to learn, but we were in business.

> *The family horse business started when Dad began to taper back his workload at the hospital. It became a very important part of my life and will continue to be.*
>
> *~ Bryan Reed*

Mary and I decided to move out to the country where we could have our own horse farm instead of boarding our horses elsewhere. We visited Kentucky barns to get a feel for what we wanted, and then we started looking around to see what was available in the Kansas City area. Finally, we found a place south of town, an old deserted homestead that had belonged to the same family since the land was homesteaded in 1837. There were eight descendants remaining and they all agreed to sell their parcels to us. We were able to buy it as one piece. The land had been divided up and was full of old barbed wire fencing and rubbish, but we cleared it all up. We left the old dry stack stone fence that had been built around the time of the Civil War but pulled the wire fences out, then laid out the road, lanes and paddocks. We built a graceful house that immediately seemed married to the land. We finished the barn in 1994, bought four mares that were in foal, hired an on-site farm manager, and our dream became a reality. We named the place after the ancient limestone bluffs on which it sits: Stonecrest Farm.

> *I started to look for something outside of surgery; you've got to find something else. On the weekend I'd go out and ride around on a tractor. Bill felt the same leanings as I did. He did it first rate, which is how he does everything. When Bill bought the land and built Stonecrest, he went back to Kentucky to see how it was done. Then he had the wood for the fencing brought in from Kentucky, and the barn and house designed with the same look and feel of horse country. For a local Kansas City guy to have a Derby third placer, that's phenomenal. He's got a beautiful place . . . the result of his hard work.*
>
> ~ Bill Hamaker, MD

If you scanned a list of the horses we've bred and owned, it might look like you were reading a syllabus for a college literature or geography course. Many of our horses are named for characters in poetry or for the places we've fished. We've got Little Giddings, The Wanderings of Oisin, Leaf-treader, Good-Hearted Woman, Googleado, Wilson River, Midvail, Dr. Hage, Mount Oread, and Tower Canyon among many, many others.

Naming a horse is serious business. By February of their yearling year, the formal name is chosen. Our horses' names come from things that are personal and important to us—they're not just an indicator of the horse's pedigree, although that is the more traditional approach. It's typical to incorporate some part of the names of the father and mother to create a hybrid version for the baby.

One of our farm's first foals was born on April 8, 1994. Martin named him Proven Cure, pulling from his father's name, Cure the Blues. Cure was the second most successful race horse out of Stonecrest Farm. His talent was as a sprinter. He ran eighty-five races and won or placed in forty-one of them, with total earnings at about $750 thousand. At age twelve, Cure won the Little Bit Lively Stake, a race done annually at Lone Star Park in Texas. He was the only twelve year-old winner of this type of high-level stakes race in thirty years. When you consider that in human years, it's the equivalent of a sixty-year old man winning a sprint at an Olympic qualifying competition—and setting a track record while doing it. Proven Cure was that kind of horse.

Dyani was our best race mare ever. She was always leisurely out the gate and five or six lengths behind by the second turn. She'd be up to the back end of the front horses by the far turn, then she'd start kicking it in at the quarter pole at the top of the stretch and she'd be flying down the lane. She was picking up all the crap from the other horses but she'd be flying, almost literally flying down the lane. If you tried to change her style, she'd not have it. They have their habits and their own way of doing things.

Can you imagine what racing is like for a horse? All the mud and sand and dirt being thrown up . . . she's got to breathe through her nose, inhaling that stuff into her lungs while she's running like her life depends on it. If someone was throwing mud in your face, could you do your best, on the fly all the way around the racetrack? Some horses aren't up to it, but some fulfill all the hopes you put into its careful breeding and hundreds of hours of training.

Most people buy their way into the racing society—they'll buy a horse for a million dollars. Dr. Reed didn't buy his way in, he's earned his place and invested wisely, and he got lucky. He's had a lot of success. He's earned a spot in the Breeder's Cup. I've been lucky enough to get to break some horses for Dr. Reed. One was a two year-old who was a bit of a juvenile delinquent that Reed named Proven Cure. That horse ended up earning $750 thousand for him. I bought a mare for him named Nice Gal. I also connected the Reeds to some of the trainers I admire. The Reeds met with them and thought they were all good. When they went out to check out Murray Johnson's place, he had little kids running around in diapers, and of all things, that clinched the deal. They hired him.

Dr. Reed asked my advice so for each of his mares I'd suggest five or six stallions for breeding. I recall a time that he contacted me when I was down in Jamaica teaching at the Mission School where I volunteered my time. I had to reply from down there. He called back and asked, "Where are you?" I told him about the charitable work I was doing, how it was something I had wanted to do since my own kids were grown, and I sent him a picture. The Reeds then sent a check for the school that covered tuition for every child plus the operation of that school for a whole year. Then Mrs. Reed also sent a check to an orphanage there. The local priest who taught at an elementary school in the Parish there asked how I'd come by such a generous benefactor. I explained who the Reeds were, and how I'd gone with Dr. Reed to watch Dynaformer, who was Perfect Drift's sire, breed a mare. The priest replied that it was going to be hard to go back to his school and explain to the families and staff that a horse's sex life was responsible for our little parish getting all this money. We still laugh about that. Reed is just an all-around great guy.

~ William Wofford, Rimroc Farm owner and professional horse trainer

Googleado, one of our best sprinters, could start off easy then finish quickly. We made sure in his training he learned to go slowly in the beginning because he always wanted to head straight for the front. It's deadly to be on the lead because you're a target. The horse that breaks out of the gate fast might fool you for a race or two. They'll be way out front by the far turn but at the quarter pole they're tiring. If you've got a horse you can "rate" –allow you to slow them down a little bit—then he'll have something to finish with. If your horse has the requisite speed and a good rider to pace him, then you've got the strength in the end that you need. It's like holding the hundred meter dash at the end of a four-hundred meter race. Googleado could do it . . . he did it easy.

Bill has a love of beautiful horses that can run. When he sees a fine horse, especially one like Perfect Drift, running well, I mean whether it's a horse or a human heart—any living organic unit that's really working well, running to perfection— that's what inspires him. It's the same goal he has had in every surgical procedure he's ever done, and in every other aspect of his life, to get as close to perfection as he can.

~ Jo Jeanne Callaway, MD

Of course, our horses are part of the family whether they're racers or not. Ka Dish Day was a little colt born on the day our friend Edna died. Edna and her husband George never had children of their own, and they loved coming out to see the new baby horses in the paddocks. When Edna got sick with breast cancer, she would come out to the farm to watch the colts and fillies . . . it gave her great peace. Bryan found his name in the Lakota-Sioux language— Ka Dish Day means "Farewell until we meet again." After she passed, George continued to visit Ka Dish Day. Our trainer Garrett let George groom him. When Ka Dish Day won his first race, we sent George a picture of the moment. But Ka Dish Day just didn't like racing, so after that first win we brought him back to the farm. He's living out his days now at Stonecrest Farm. And George still comes to see him.

The Reed family views horseracing as a beautiful sport in which the horse always comes first . . . ahead of anything else. If the horse has a minor ailment, that gets dealt with as a priority over racing. Ninety-five percent of owners would run it, but the Reeds would rather have a sound horse. They always do the right thing by the horse.

There was a big chestnut horse, a real tough one to deal with, that Dr. Reed named after his brother: Brother Lowell. We ran him and he was short on talent but long on heart. We had issues with him until the point where he wasn't competing at the level he needed to be. Most owners would have put him in a claim race just to get rid of him. The Reeds wouldn't do that. Instead, they found him a good home where a little girl is riding him. The Reeds treat all their horses like Perfect Drift . . . even if they can't outrun me in over-boots, they're still treated like Tom Brady. Most owners don't care, and use various ways to get rid of a horse. At Stonecrest Farm, we breed our horses carefully and race them. When their racing days are over, the Reeds bring them back to Stonecrest or find a good home for them. The game would be better if more people were like Dr. Reed.

~ Garrett Smith, Stonecrest Farm Manager

Some owners would get rid of a horse like Ka Dish Day, but we don't see things that way at Stonecrest. Mary in particular views our horse farm holistically. Her sensitivity to the horse's experience is a given, but she sees a lot more at the racetrack than most people would take in, starting with life on the "Backside." The Backside of a racetrack is where the nitty gritty goes on, from walking the horses to mucking out their stalls. The service people who live and work there are invisible to the crowds—out of sight and mind. Their lives are centered on racing culture, but not the cultured part of it. There's nothing glamorous about it. There are drugs and alcohol. The children of the Backside people dart around like waifs. Where do they live? Do they attend school? Mary worries about them. If she could load them into our car and bring them home with us, I'm sure she would. It might still happen. We have contributed sizably to the racetrack chaplaincy that jockey Pat Day established to help the Backside people.

Mary's influence has also played a role in the selection of jockeys. The etiquette is to choose the rider because he fits the horse. The rider has an agent, and the agent's job is to get the best horse for his rider in a particular race. Mary's strategy is to look for the winningest jockeys who don't whip the horses, she just won't stand for that— none of us will. A jockey can be set down for excessive use of crop. Even though today's shorter crops don't injure them, some horses resent it. A real aggressive rider will overuse the crop. It's terrible to watch. You'll find that Hall of Fame jockeys like Gary Stevens, Pat Day, and Eddie Delahoussaye get to the top of the heap without whipping the horse. In fact, you rarely find an aggressive rider at the top. We've had some of the best riders there are on our horses including Eddie Delahoussaye. Pat Day rode Perfect Drift for a year and a half without ever hitting him with a crop, not one time. He told me, "Dr. Reed, the horse is giving you what he can give you, there's no point in punishing him for doing that."

*C*ozinette was a real mean bitch mare, but Mary loved her. She was different, and Mary recognized that everyone was rejecting her because of her personality. Mary is always the one who reaches out to the outsider and the underdog—like turning a feral cat into a pet—Mary does that kind of thing. Mary has a loving way with our quirky, difficult horses, and they absolutely love her in return. Mary's patient attention was gentling . . . a kind of therapy for Cozinette.

Cozy Lass was Cozinette's daughter, a beautiful gray mare like her mother, but she didn't look like she could do much on the race track. Cozy Lass was bred to run on grass not dirt, but our trainer felt she needed to have track experience. We took her to Chicago's Hawthorne Park without any great expectations. She was entered in a grass race, but because of heavy rain the event was moved to a sloppy dirt track. She broke slowly, but on this day, Cozy Lass finally started getting interested in racing as she reached the far turn. When she got to the quarter pole, she was way, way behind, ten lengths or more. But then she started running like crazy down the lane and she ended up winning. Cozy Lass won again that year then took the winter off.

In the spring, we were at Churchill Downs to race Cozy Lass again. It was a "claiming race" which means an owner or licensed trainer can buy any horse in it for a set amount of money, which in this case was forty thousand. If you run your horse in a claiming race, you do so knowing it could be sold. Cozy was an Illinois-bred horse and our trainer didn't think anybody would be interested. However, Cozy won that race, and sure enough, she was claimed. Mary was heartbroken over that, and immediately went about getting her back. She learned that whoever claimed her had already resold her. Mary was terribly distraught to think we'd lost Cozy forever. Indeed, it took me four years to pull it off, but finally I told Mary I found the guy who had her. It was one of those moments a husband lives for—making his wife truly happy. Mary looked up at me with cautious hope in her eyes and asked if we could talk to him about getting

Cozy back. I said, "You're already talking to him . . . I've just bought your horse back for you."

After we got Cozy Lass back, she became a breeding mare. She had her first baby, and then a second. It was during that foaling that Cozy died from a ruptured uterus. We were heartbroken. Her baby was a filly, so we named her Cozy's Promise. Promise was a good race horse, a sprinter, and she was headed to high level winning. She was coming up odds-on favorite in her next race, but her neck and throat started swelling the night before she was set to run. She had an acute pharyngitis that obstructed her breathing and almost killed her. Promise lost part of her vocal chords in surgery, but she survived. Her racing days behind her, Promise became a breeding mare and lives at Stonecrest Farm today.

*I*n raising and racing horses, you're hoping for the one that is raring to go and loves competition. Some horses are just born for it, which is why so much effort goes into the breeding. A winning stud and mare are no guarantee of success in the baby, but it sure worked that way for us in 2002. We've been lucky to have some amazing horses over the years, but so far the best of them has been Perfect Drift.

In April 1999, Perfect Drift was born at Wayfare Farm in Lexington, Kentucky. He was a Bay, the son of Nice Gal, one of our mares that we bred to his sire, Dynaformer. One can never be totally sure about the talents of the offspring, but in breeding, you're attempting to imbue qualities from the stallion and mare that you want in the foal. Dynaformer brought size and toughness. Nice Gal brought speed and staying power. Bryan picked out his name, Perfect Drift. It was inspired by that exquisite moment in fly fishing when you cast your fly and it's floating perfectly down a river into the spot where you know the fish are feeding. It comes from reading the water. It might look effortless, but a lot goes into achieving a perfect drift, and so the name was very apropos.

As a baby, Drift looked plain but full of potential—good bone with a good bit of attitude. You want that kind of spirit in competition. Mike Frederickson was our Stonecrest Farm manager back then. He began training Drift during the spring of 2001. He told me Perfect Drift had something different . . . he had *presence*. Even the way that horse stood said *look at me*. He thrived in training and had unique athletic ability. Drift grew strong shouldered with muscled hips, a powerful neck, and a well-balanced head. He had a little white s-curve under his forelock. His mane was thick and dark, and his tail went all the way to the ground. By his two year-old year, Perfect Drift was a magnificent horse.

Stonecrest Farm has some of the best thoroughbreds in this part of the country. When they need a vet, he brings them over. I am a thoroughbred enthusiast myself, so it was so heartwarming to hear Dr. Reed talk about his anticipation for Perfect Drift. He'd run a few races really well, but you can't get too excited about anything. Things can change direction, so Reed was understated but very excited.

In the thoroughbred world, to be able to go and buy a beautiful horse and take it straight to the track is one way to do it. The other way is when you own the mare, pick the stallion, and then watch that foal grow and run around your pastures. If it shows some promise, you take it to the track and enter bigger and bigger races. That's the way it worked for Perfect Drift. The Reeds love that horse and it worked so well. They never pushed him, and he gave everything he could give. For him to race Grade One Stakes, to be the winner of four and a half million dollars, it was just amazing to be able to see that all happen.

~ *Beth Davis, DVM, Professor,*
Section Head Equine Medicine and Surgery, PhD,
Board Certified ACVIM, Kansas State University College of
Veterinary Medicine, Dept. of Clinical Sciences,
The Veterinary Health Center, Kansas State University

At Churchill Downs on November 16, 2001, Perfect Drift ran his first race. It looked like he was going to win that one, but a horse beat him right at the wire. True to form, Drift reached over and tried to bite him. The second race was in December at Turfway Park. He broke from the starting gate and made the lead easily. Drift was two or three lengths ahead of the other horses when he started slowing down. I thought, oh gosh, he's going to give it in, but he heard the horses come up behind him, and Drift came back again. He won easily. This was his "maiden race," which means the first race he won.

When I got home that night, I had a call from an agent who was trying to buy prospects—meaning potential Kentucky Derby horses. He offered me $450 thousand for Perfect Drift. I said I'd get back to him, and then told my trainer Murray Johnson about it. Murray shook his head and told me it was going to be really hard for a horse to run out $450 thousand. I came home and put it to the family. They all responded unanimously. We didn't go into this for the money, we did it for the racing . . . for being in it together. So we stayed in it, we didn't sell him. Thank God we didn't.

> *Whether it's about horses or the hospital, my in-laws are always about the greater good. What can they do to bring the family together and share in an experience? When he talks about Perfect Drift, he doesn't talk about wins and money, Dad talks about how the horse took us to a whole lot of fun places together. All the trips we took, even with extended family, it was about how that experience gave the family something to share together.*
>
> ~ *Rita Reed, Jeff's wife*

The Preview was the next race Perfect Drift won, also at Turfway Park. He finished second in the following two races behind a horse named Request for Parole. These were progressively longer races, which meant that Drift could "get the distance" experience. We needed more than a sprinter, as Murray put it, we needed more distance. With each race, Drift showed his promise. His one weakness was that if he took the lead down the stretch, he'd get a little cocky like he already won. But Perfect Drift continued to climb the prospect ladder until he qualified for horseracing's finest event, the Kentucky Derby.

> *Dad and I have different tastes in the conformation of horses, but we have learned that we can both be right or wrong in assessing talent. We all experience the wins and losses in our own way. In fact, I watched many of Perfect Drift's races off on my own and continue to do so when I am at a race where one of our horses is competing. I do remember the night after winning the Spiral Stakes—the race that sent Perfect Drift on to the Kentucky Derby. We both couldn't sleep and went over to see the horse at four in the morning.*
>
> ~ *Bryan Reed*

*I*t was the first Saturday in May 2002 and the Reed family was at Churchill Downs for the Kentucky Derby. We'd gone in a week ahead for all the festivities and dinners. As the race got closer, we could hardly sleep. We would go down to the barn to see Drift and talk to him. On the morning of the race, we were at the track by ten o'clock. The ladies had their hats on and we were all dressed to the nines. We made our way to the Grandstand where box seats are reserved for the owners. Mary stayed there while the boys, Dianne and I went down to the barn to wait for the Walkover.

Of all the thrills we've known in horseracing, the Kentucky Derby Walkover had to be the high point. The Walkover is when the trainers, owners, and family escort their horse from the backstretch barns through the chute and into the procession around the arena. This is Churchill Downs at its finest—all the pageantry of thoroughbred racing culture with 160 thousand fans cheering at a fevered pitch from every conceivable point in, around, and behind the stadium that affords a view. Everything looks beautiful and feels hopeful—things could go our way, which every owner is no doubt thinking. Television crews from countries far and wide are reporting live to people watching across the globe—no matter the language, you can hear and understand the fervor in the reporters' voices. The atmosphere is so exuberant that your heart nearly beats out of your chest. There are people everywhere from the rooftops to the grass. Photographers are lying on the ground along the railing so they can capture the horses coming around and into view. It's an incredible feeling to be part of this tradition that goes back to 1875. The anticipation is intense but optimistic. No one has won or lost yet; everything seems possible. The horses parade regally out to the saddling paddocks, and that is the Walkover. Bob Baffert, a world-renowned trainer who has several Kentucky Derby wins under his belt, likens the Walkover to the gladiators circling the arena in Rome.

Even though we were from Kansas City, the locals treated us like adopted-hometown heroes because Drift was bred in Kentucky; he'd done a lot of training at the Churchill Downs Training Center. Given the number of the horses racing that day that weren't of Kentucky stock, I guess we were more at home at Churchill Downs than some. Still, Stonecrest was a Missouri farm, and we knew full well that the Show-Me state was watching with a special pride. In truth, all kinds of people from everywhere in the world had been watching these horses, including Drift, from the time they were two year-olds. All eyes were now fixed on the Derby.

In the few moments we still had with Perfect Drift before the race, Bryan tucked a little heart-shaped charm into his saddle cloth. It was like the one given to the Tin Man by the Wizard of Oz. We all touched our horse reverently and said things with our hearts to him, and he to us. Then it was time. We rushed with as much dignity as possible back to our box. Ten minutes before the gate, "Riders Up" was called and the jockeys mounted the horses. They paraded out in sequence. As soon as the first horse emerged onto the racetrack, the band began playing My Old Kentucky Home. Everybody stood and sang, half the crowd was crying. It was an enormous moment that would be followed by the two most exciting minutes in racing known as The Kentucky Derby.

> *It started in '92. I could drive up to Nashville to Louisville or Lexington and see a few races. Woodlands would show them simulcast. Dad took us to the biggest races all across the country. They were just small-time affairs until Perfect Drift. When he came along, it was so much fun we could go to Saratoga, to the Pacific Class. Drift was in a lot of big races. It was a lot of fun to be there. It's so neat to see your horse and your silks and colors coming around that stretch—your horse being such a celebrity. People knew our silks because Drift was racing year in and year out for eight years. He had a huge fan base. It was a lot of fun riding the coattails of that horse. The feeling of being a part of the Kentucky Derby, wow . . . there's nothing like it.*
>
> *~ Martin Reed*

The section where the owners sit has an excellent view from the Grand Stand just above the finish line. The horses were approaching the starting gate just as we got to our box. The air around us throttled with vibrancy. I thought Drift could win; his odds were eight to one. He'd been picked by one of the broadcasters, so he was highly regarded. Even if he didn't win, we all felt incredibly proud just to be a part of the Derby, an event author John Steinbeck called "an emotion, a turbulence, an explosion."

The starting bell sounded exactly like the air felt—bursting with excitement. The horses launched out of their gates. I watched our jockey Eddie Delahoussaye maneuver Drift ahead and couldn't believe he brought him so close to the front . . . risky. They rounded the first turn and War Emblem was in the lead, Drift was running third. I looked at my family—their faces exhilarated. We were yelling like crazy. In the home stretch, Proud Citizen, the horse in second place, moved over in front of Drift so Eddie had to slow us down a bit. There was no space to get around Proud Citizen now, and all three horses held their positions as they had from the start. Even though we could see that we weren't going to win, it was thrilling to watch our horse flying at the front of that formation with so much grit and grace. Perfect Drift came in third, and we were so proud of him. Our jockey and horse were safe, and the best effort had been given. It was not only enough, it was more than we'd ever hoped for . . . we were elated.

*P*erfect Drift was a true competitor. In a race, he never got sweaty or anxious at all. He'd come over dancing a bit and alert, ears forward, taking in the scene, always on his toes. When he got into the race, if a horse bumped him, it didn't bother or intimidate him, he just went on with it. He loved the race itself. In fact, Drift was so competitive that being behind out of the gate was sometimes an advantage. I'll never forget when were at the Whitney, a million dollar race at Saratoga in the fall of his four year-old year. Half way through the race, Drift was ten lengths behind all the other horses. He picked up his pace and got ahead of every horse but one. Our jockey, Pat Day, made the lead a hundred yards from the finish, so Drift relaxed because he thought he had it won. But right at the end, the other horse beat Drift by a nose. Pat came up to me afterwards and apologized, "Dr. Reed, you got beat today by an impatient jockey. I know we'd have won that race if I hadn't made the lead so soon." The rider who knew our horse knew Drift's tendency towards cockiness.

Perfect Drift kept on racing. Our first enormous win was in The Stephen Foster. He was the only horse in history that qualified five times in a row for the world championship of horseracing, The Breeder's Cup Classic. When he was a four year-old, he ran it in

California but had a particularly heartbreaking loss. The horses were leaning into the rail, and Funny Cide, who won the Kentucky Derby in 2003, was immediately inside of Drift. At the first turn, Funny Cide went straight, forcing Drift far to the outside, which put us right out of the race. Although Drift made a huge effort to overcome that, he just couldn't. When Murray Johnson brought him back to the barn, Drift kept his head out the window and his butt to the entrance of his stall. He didn't want to see any of us. He was pissed off, you could tell. Believe me, racehorses know when they win or lose.

Perfect Drift continued to be an odds-on favorite, but he cracked his cannon bone when he was an eight year-old in 2007, so we had to sit him out for a while. Another time, we scratched Drift out of a million dollar race in California because he had a small corneal ulcer. I had the vet look at him before Drift was put on the plane. The vet said it wasn't looking as good as he'd like, but it wouldn't affect the race. I said let's scrap it. I wouldn't play one of my own boys on a bad ankle.

Perfect Drift finally retired in his nine year-old year. By the time he was through racing, Perfect Drift had won $4,714,213.00, making him the second richest racehorse in North America at that time. In May 2014, the *Courier Journal* on-line reported, "Perfect Drift ran fifty times, with eleven wins, fourteen seconds and seven thirds. He ran in the Breeders' Cup Classic five times, including finishing third in 2005. The gelding was a fixture in Churchill Downs' stakes for older horses, including taking the Grade I Stephen Foster Handicap by a head over eventual Horse of the Year Mineshaft."

Even though his racing years are behind him, I think Perfect Drift still wants to race. He's still full of spirit and personality. That horse has attitude. If a guy walks by his stall, Drift might take a piece out of him, even if that guy is me. But he's gentle with the ladies. If a woman walks by his stall, he'll nuzzle her. You could put a handicapped person in a wheelchair right in his stall without a worry. Drift's awareness of the disabled, of children, and of females was uncanny and entirely compassionate. He's always loved women more than men, particularly my daughter-in-law, Dianne.

> *Some of my favorite memories come from race trips. Bryan, Dad and I followed Perfect Drift all over the country before his retirement. We met lots of interesting people who wanted to talk horses as much as we did. Probably my favorite spot we visited was Delmar. I was the one to pick out restaurants and we had some wonderful meals together. Early mornings at the track with coffee were a great way to start the day.*
>
> *~ Dianne Reed, Bryan's wife*

> *After he stopped racing, Perfect Drift became a live exhibit at the Churchill Downs Museum. He was there for fans to take pictures with, and just be admired. But Drift is very athletic; he needs to be used. Essentially, he got fired from his job because the museum staff said they couldn't handle him. Now he's learning to be track horse. The track or pony horse leads the horses out for races, and Drift has to learn that he's not going to race. He's doing very well so far. The plan for Perfect Drift is to stay at Churchill Downs during the meet, or he might come back here and help the other two year-olds out at Stonecrest. That's what my mom wants him to do.*
>
> *~ Martin Reed*

Perfect Drift was at the Kentucky Derby again in 2014, but this time it was as pony horse. Drift was selected to escort California Chrome during warm-ups right before the race. "Given who (Perfect Drift) is, and the horse that is the favorite for the Kentucky Derby, I felt like he has the right to take the favorite. He deserves that spot," said Monnie Goetz in a May 2014 interview featured in the *Courier Journal* on-line. Goetz is a veteran horsewoman in charge of the racetrack pony operation at Churchill Downs. She retrained Perfect Drift for his second career mentoring the younger horses training there, and she's still got a special place for Drift in her heart. Monnie explained, "He's very loved in Kentucky. When they find out who he is, everybody wants to pet him and give him some attention. You hear so much about him. He's a little special, always has been. A horse who has run that many times in the Breeders' Cup, how can you not have him lead him out?" *(Jennie Rees, USA TODAY Sports; May 3, 2014 in the Courier Journal on-line)*

I'd like to think our horse gets some of the credit for California Chrome's win in 2014 . . . that our Drift was sharing some trade secrets as he led Chrome around the track.

Dr. Reed's number one objective is taking the best possible care of his horses. Even if the horse isn't capable of winning, he still gives that horse the best possible life. Here at Kansas State University, we maintain a small herd to teach our veterinary students the basic skills. Bill and Mary Reed have been strong supporters of our program. In fact, one of the horses in our teaching herd was donated by the Reeds. Their philanthropy is notable and extremely generous. Dr. Reed established The Mary Reed Equine Compassion Fund, a $25,000 grant to the school. Scholarships from that fund are awarded annually to veterinary students at Kansas State who exemplify compassionate care. Also, we have a group of equine specialists training in internal medicine, surgery, and reproduction that Dr. Reed provides support to that's invaluable. We're so limited in state dollars to pay salaries for vets in training, so this takes a huge burden off them and ensures that they receive the support to get their training. He also stays in close touch with our equine section as a medical professional—always asking if there are things he could do to help us. He's been so generous and helpful in providing our students with awards and scholarships. The Reeds are a truly remarkable people.

~ Beth Davis, DVM

Thoroughbreds have well-documented stories called pedigrees, and Stonecrest Farm is a storied place. Perfect Drift was a Cinderella story, but for every fairy tale there have been several more tales with sadder endings . . . the year we lost two promising fillies, Hallett and 26-I-Knows, when they were struck by lightning out in the meadow; the year a weanling ran into a fence and broke her shoulder. When our retired thoroughbred, Dr. Hage, was at the end of his long life, our trainer Garrett's son Jaxson held the horse's head in his lap and couldn't be convinced by his dad to go on up to the house. He was about nine years old then, and Jaxson has grown up around horses so they are probably more important to him than his buddies at school. I watched this little boy kneel in the tall grass and stay with the horse until it was over. He prayed for Dr. Hage to go to heaven. It was like seeing my son Bryan when he was a little guy. I still get choked up thinking about it.

All of my boys loved animals, but Bryan in particular responded to them with a sense of calling. He grew up and became a veterinarian. He is often requested when it's time to put an animal down. Bryan does this in a way that dignifies the animal's life and the bond between it and the owner. He told Mary and me about a house call he once made out at a trailer where a leathery biker lived . . . how he gently euthanized the guy's dog as it sat in its favorite spot in the world—in front of his owner on the motorcycle. The biker just held his dog gently and talked to him until he fell asleep. Bryan is the vet you call for that kind of compassionate service.

Jeff and his dad have this little thing they do. Whenever we're driving together through the gates up to the farm, it'll be a contest to see who will say, "Gee, I wonder who lives here?" first. Actually, we all know it's my father-in-law's line, but everybody feels this way about Stonecrest. It's just a magical place.

~ Rita, Jeff's wife

Stonecrest Farm continues to be a working horse farm but also a retreat and respite for our family and friends. Every evening after a long day at the hospital, I'd drive through the gates of the farm and feel I was leaving the world of worries behind. People who come out to see us have told us the farm has the same effect on them. Mary and I recognize our stewardship of the horses also extends to this place, so we open it up to others in many ways. Stonecrest Farm has housed people who needed a place to come away from the world for a while. Many have stayed with us during some kind of transition in their lives. We host a day-camp in the summer for kids from the inner-city, and regularly bring various groups out for special events, charitable fundraising, tours, and any other thing we can do to share the peaceful feeling of this place with others.

Stonecrest Farm is the culmination of dreams.

~ Jeff Reed

A yearling at Stonecrest Farm in 2013

CHAPTER 10

Equine Theologian

The wind of heaven is that which blows between a horse's ears.

~ Arabian Proverb

Here's what I can tell you about what I have learned from raising horses. They are willing teachers for any ready student, and that's certainly who I am. What surprised me the most was how alike horses and people are. They have to understand what you want them to do . . . if they trust you and feel encouragement from you, they'll do it. That's as true for a human being as a horse. Horses appreciate your presence as much as you appreciate theirs. In general, women are wonderful with horses. Bryan's wife Dianne is warm and trusting . . . horses love her.

Training horses requires a great deal of patience and it takes an expert trainer to accurately read them. There's no forcing a horse to do anything. You can be running the best horses, but if you push them to do something before they're ready to do it, it'll mess with their brain and they'll be no good on the racetrack. Of course, some horses aren't racers. They get all nervous and sweaty, "washing out" at the racetrack. There's no changing that. They may have been bred for running but they're just not made for racing.

Horses have individual personalities and inclinations just like people do. Some are nice, some mean, and some are just misunderstood. There's a difference between a horse that's mean and a horse that has an attitude. Attitudes are innate . . . a matter of breeding and spirit. Meanness results from bad experiences—usually with people. Those horses need careful handling—they respond to gentleness but they're wary and mistrustful. Who could blame them?

Horses can read your mood with a sensitivity that's uncanny. They have a body language that's unmistakable, but it takes a lot of experience to get all the nuances of it with any individual horse . . . the small talk of nostrils, ear twitches and head bobs. There is a communication I experience with some horses that leaves me feeling I've had a deep discussion with a trusted friend . . . and I've gotten some very good advice. It uplifts and inspires me. It calms and replenishes me. I will say this: horses are healers in their own way, and I have been their satisfied patient.

One of the old sayings in the horse world is, "No trainer ever commits suicide with an unraced two year-old in his barn." You live on hope, and whether the horse is a competitor or just not meant for the track, the husbandry of horses has its own rewards. It's a different kind of fulfillment than medicine, but it still has to do with healing. In both, you're dealing with the eternal things . . . the life of another living being and how you can affect that in a positive way. That's been my life's mission. It's about growing into who I was meant to be, and giving myself to that cause. My appreciation of these wonderful animals that God placed on this earth . . . the privilege of being around them . . . it's a thing that feeds me. This magnificent creature that nods its head and reaches out to be fed is in fact nourishing me. There is a reciprocal exchange between humans and horses that gives both of us something we need to be alive.

Most of my colleagues who struggled with depression and stress-related issues were those who had nothing but their work. Upon retirement, they left the hospital without a further purpose to their life. Their entire identity was tied to their profession, so retirement left them feeling like life was over. For me, horses have given my life a balance it very much needed, as well as another way to explore what it means to be truly alive. Sometimes you can go out to the barn or the paddock and feel a connection with a horse that you can't afford to fully indulge in other aspects of your life.

My colleague Bill Hamaker had a farm not far from Stonecrest where he kept show horses many years ago. He had a mare that died foaling. He told me he just sat down and cried. Here's a tough guy who was in Vietnam watching guys jump out of helicopters to their death and it was this horse that brought him to tears. I can relate to that entirely.

For Mary and me, Stonecrest Farm is about more than horses . . . it's about connecting to something with deep meaning for both of us, and it is another way of serving and healing. It's an extension of what we feel called to do, and it gives balance to both of us. Stonecrest is a place where you come back to the well for a deep drink of peace and quiet. School kids, children with special needs, senior citizens, charitable and church groups or just people who cross our path in some way come out here to learn about horses and maybe even about themselves. The horses perk up their ears and come trotting over to the fence in hopes of a nuzzle and a peppermint. They touch their soft muzzles to whoever is there and it feels like a blessing. We share this graceful place because we both feel this is part of the stewardship of it . . . to let others take in the many kinds of beauty they find here.

I try to bring people here so I can share this farm with them. I've been blessed because I've had the opportunity to do so much. I wish I was still physically able to take care of friends when they're sick. I've always been there for someone who was sick, even my folks, but now I can't do that. I guess it's part of getting old. I'm content to just be here at Stonecrest. There's no other place I'd like to go or do. I've been there and done it already. What we have shared together and have here now is beyond my expectations. I've been really privileged to live this life.

~ Mary Reed

Fragments of a legend long-since forgotten tell of a sacred lodge painted with pictures from a vision.

Four by four horses, in four different colors: Blue Roans in honor of the Chinook, White horses for the icy northern winds, Grey horses for the sunrise, and Red Roans for the south . . .

A circle on the ground with two straight lines drawn across, one maiden in each direction holding sacred things; a bow and arrow, a holy pipe, healing herbs, a white goose feather and a flowering stick . . .

A dark cloud emerges from the west and all look up in silence. A singer sends a voice to the spirits of the cloud. Then a Blue Roan pricks his ears, raises his tail and paws the earth, neighs long and loud to the west. All the other horses join in, then all horses in the village . . .

Lightning and thunder comes from the cloud, strong winds sweeps over the lands. Hail and rain falling, only yonder but not near. The thunder spirits are joyful, coming to see the dance and hear the sacred songs . . .

The four maidens hold up the sacred things; offerings to the thunder spirits. The grandfathers beat the drums and the dance begins, the horses prancing and rearing . . .

The sad are happy again—the sick are healed.

~ Retold by The Nokota Horse Conservancy

Horses have been mythologized in every culture throughout history. I'm sure there has always been a Horse Culture in every civilization where horses and humans have shared their lives. There is a Divinity about this magnificent animal, and I don't feel the least bit irreverent sharing my own theology of horsemanship which recognizes these tenets:

- The first, most important loving relationship is between the mare and her baby; it is key to a horse's sound mind to experience the love of its mother.

- Horses recognize and establish a natural pecking order and equine-societal norms.

- Each horse has a personality with unique likes, dislikes, and habits uniquely his or her own. Gender influences behavior; expect behavioral differences between male and female horses.

- Every horse remembers any bad treatment it has received. Horses will specifically remember who treated them badly; they might even hold a grudge against anyone who reminds them of mistreatment.

- Horses have healing powers affecting one's emotional health. The trust that develops between a human and a horse can promote healing in both.

- Horses have a language all their own, and if we take the time to learn it, we'll learn the intuitive answers to some of life's mysteries. Horses know and connect . . . they sense who you are, your voice, even when you're afraid. They tune into your attitude and mood. They will communicate what they're afraid of, when they're in pain or angry or hungry.

- They'll teach you about love and loyalty. They'll give you a reason to believe in something greater than yourself.

If we listen to the horse, watch his responses, then we'll learn about trust. We reach for each other in understanding, a process that is part intuition and part experience. Patience and gentleness work better than forcing or pushing. Imagine how you would feel if someone put a steel bit in your mouth, the weight of a leather saddle on your back, and then sat astride it to ride you around. Think of how the horse feels about what you're asking of him, and the trust it takes to give in to that.

The design of a horse invites the man to ride, and ride he must. Human survival has depended on this relationship. I've wondered what the horse gets out of all this, but have to admit there seems to be some reciprocity. The horse wants to explore a trail together, to listen to you talk about your joys and concerns. But you must first earn his trust. And you must deserve a horse's faith in you. Horses give assurance, and we provide reassurance. Fluency in one another's language creates a bond in faith and trust . . . this is a very mystical healing journey a horse and human can take together.

Photo Album

I am grateful to the photographers
whose work appears here.

Most photos are from our personal collection.
If not, and the source or photographer
is known, credit has been given.

Inaccuracies or omissions
are regretted.

Special Thanks to

Leeanne Seaver

Derek Donelson, Media Clerk,
Kokomo High School, Kokomo, Indiana

Four Footed Fotos, Inc.

Ingram's, Kansas City's Business Magazine

Kansas City Star and photographers
Mark Nickel anad Tammy Ljungblad

Bill Reed in a hat stands on the porch behind his parents in the only known picture of him from boyhood. His best friend Nip is far left.

"One of the places we lived brought a substantial improvement to my life: I finally made a best friend."

Bill Reed (in tie) with his family in Kokomo, circa 1950

"High school graduation wasn't a given for kids like me, much less going onto college, so I was on the vocational track—no math, no language arts, no preparation for anything but the labor force."

Bill played Center for the Kokomo Wildcats, 1944.

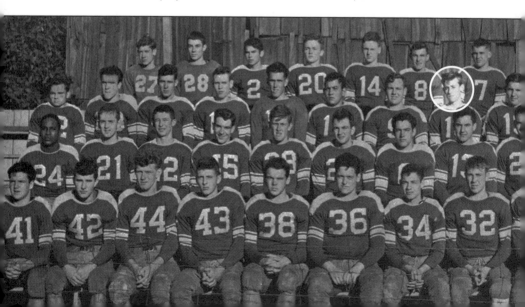

Rick (3rd child of 8), Bill (4th child) in Navy uniform, and Lowell (eldest) Reed, 1945

*"I did manage to graduate from Kokomo High School
in May of 1945 just in time to enlist for the end of
World War II."*

Bill Reed,
Kokomo High School
Yearbook, 1943

Medical school graduate
William Reed, 1954

"It was a brand new
idea and I had no
idea where it came
from, but there it was.

I wanted to be
a doctor."

Mary Shear, circa 1952

"... She was
gorgeous in her
crisp white uniform,
the starched nurse's
cap crowning her
dark hair."

Wedding Day, 1954

"… I handed her a ring and said matter of factly, 'Take this with you and set the date.' I wish I'd been more romantic, and I'm pretty sure Mary does, too."

From left—Martin, Bryan and Jeff, Edinburgh, Scotland, circa 1967

"I would do my job then come home. Family was my priority."

April 1970

The Reed
Family

Jeff, Bryan,
Bill, Martin
and Mary

Bill and Mary Reed at
the St. Luke's Heart Ball
in the early 1970's

*"I had many
'how could this be
happening to me'
moments prompted
by experiences and
material possessions
that I never could
have imagined
as a boy."*

With then Vice President
Gerald Ford and
Kansas Representative
Larry Winn in 1973.

Bill and brother Jay, circa 1968

Bryan, Jeff, Bill and Martin Reed
flyfishing in Alaska in the early
1980s.

The Reed family at Bryan and Dianne's wedding in 1991.

"Mary was effusive in her love of our boys."

STAR☆

SUNDAY MAGAZINE OF THE KANSAS CITY STAR

OCTOBER 30, 1977

Home
Secti

An Affair of the Heart   page 10

Cover, *Kansas City STAR Magazine*
October 30, 1977

"You could be the best surgeon ever to grace the planet, but your patient could still die if you weren't fast enough."

Transplant at St. Luke's

By The Star's staff

A 60-year-old Savannah, Mo., man today became the ninth person to receive a heart transplant at Mid America Heart Institute of St. Luke's Hospital in Kansas City.

Eugene Wilmes was in critical but stable condition today after an operation Sunday night lasting about 2 hours and 20 minutes, a hospital spokesman said.

The spokesman said Wilmes was suffering from ischemic cardiomyopathy, a condition causing the the heart to enlarge and weaken. His operation started at 10:20 p.m and was performed by transplant surgeon Dr. William Reed of the Institute, the spokesman said.

The first heart transplant at the Institute was performed in June 1985.

Here are the surgeons heart transplants to Kan

By Connie Brockert

FOUR HEART transplants were performed in Kansas City last year, and that number will probably at least double this year. Technical and surgical proce surgery out of the r tal. It now is an a those with specific and, for them, it although not certa to their lives.

Cardiac patients lent medical institu and three of them programs, although St. Luke's, has not plant. KANSAS C with the transpla whom made it clea of a large team. members the publi ures pushing the And ultimately, t determine whether successful.

Dr. William A. Reed
St. Luke's Hospital

Since the early 1970s, St. Luke's Hos tal has had the largest cardiovascular pi

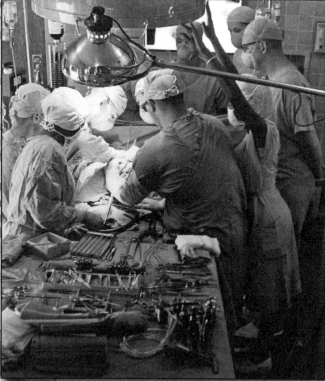

many things about cyclospori (the ant rejection drug) that we still don't know a well as other long-term consequences consider. And the patients, as with other cardiac operations, have to make drastic changes in their lifestyles."

Reed says his team is studying tech niques and theories from around the coun try. Transplants will become a major commitment at St. Luke's, which plans to add a surgeon with special transplant expertise. Reed already performs six to cardiac surgeries a week and will not be able to give full time to the transplant program.

Before joining St. Luke's in 1971, Reed 57, was Chief of Cardiovascular Surgery at Kansas University Medical Center. He went to medical school at Indiana University

'I still feel a thrill when see the human heart egin to beat again.'

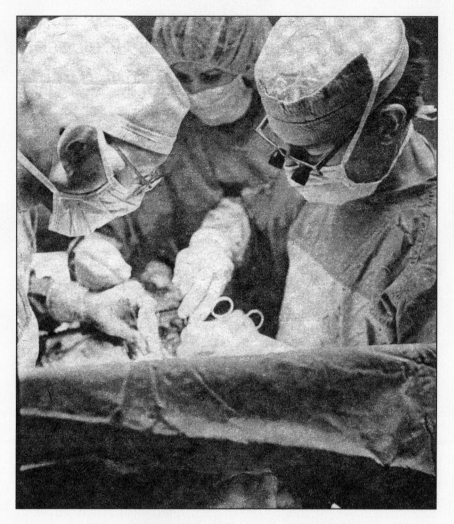

Above – Dr. Reed (right) performs surgery with help from
scrub nurse Elaine (Hollenbeck) Russell (center).
Reprinted with permission from the *Kansas City Star Magazine*, October 30, 1977

Opposite – Dr. Reed in surgery at the University of Kansas Hospital, circa 1961.
Courtesy of KUMC Archive

Opposite background – From *Kansas City* publication, February 1985

William A. Reed, MD
University of Kansas Hospital

14, 2007

Ingram's – Kansas City's Business Magazine, February/2007, featuring Heroes in Healthcare, including Bill Reed. Reprinted with permission.

Above – Bill Reed (right) tours the Center for Advanced Heart Care at the University of Kansas Hospital with colleague, John Florio. The facility's surgical center will be named for Reed and his wife, Mary. From the *Kansas City Star Magazine*, January 8, 2006

in care .007

172

Mary and Bill at Stonecrest Farm, 1998

"By late 1980s, my sons were older, married and pursuing their own interests. I wanted to find something we could all do together ... That's how one of the greatest joys of my life began ... raising and racing thoroughbreds."

The Reed family in 2004 – (From left) Martin, Dianne, Bryan, Mary, Bill, Jeff and Rita.

Above – Perfect Drift (left) and Proven Cure (right) enjoy their retirement from racing at Stonecrest Farm, 2014.

Bill and Mary's granddaughter Emily, daughter of Bryan and Dianne Reed.

Rita and Jeff Reed with sons Joey and Justin.

Left – Proven Cure winning at Churchill Downs, circa 1997.

Below – Perfect Drift was like lightning in a bottle. Shown here rounding the first turn in the Kentucky Derby, he is second from right. *2002 Photos courtesy of Four Footed Fotos*

"Everything looks beautiful and feels hopeful—things could go our way, which every owner is no doubt thinking."

Reliving some of Stonecrest Farm's wins

The Reed family and the Stonecrest Farm race team enjoy a moment of Perfect Drift triumph at the Hawthorne Gold Cup, 2003. *Photo courtesy of Four Footed Fotos*

"...it became abundanty clear that horses would be much

Mary Reed (in red) and Friends of the Mounted Patrol including Margaret Lyddon,
Mary Ellen Purucker, Sylvia Hartwig, Rhea Winslow, Sgt. Joey Roberts and Alice Lee.

*" … Mary Reed deserves the lion's share of the credit for making
the Kansas City Mounted Patrol viable. She created a foundation to
raise money and keep them funded. She believes in the power of
horses to calm people down … She's right about that."* Garrett Smith

more than a hobby for us—they became a way of life."

Mary Reed welcomes visitors to Stonecrest Farm for a tour and a talk.

The house at Stonecrest Farm is surrounded by paddocks and woods.

"Whenever we're driving together through the gates up to the farm,
it'll be a contest to see who will say,
'Gee, I wonder who lives here?' first …
It's just a magical place."

Bill Reed and Perfect Drift at Stonecrest Farm
Photo from the *Kansas City Star Magazine*, January 8, 2006

*"I've wondered what the horse gets out of all this ...
this is a very mystical healing journey a horse and human
can take together."*

10-6-10

Dear Dr. Reed,

Just a note to bring you up to date on one of your successes. I'm now eighty-four years old and still enjoying an active life style. I had a myocardial infarct at age forty-three and in 1983 you performed a quadruple bypass on me. In 1997 _____ balloon angioplasty _____ _____ artery. _____ _____ because _____

10/19/13

Stonecrest Farm

Dear Leeanne,

Colors changing here they must be there. Thank you for staying _____ Redding some day about John Updike. He wrote that happiness has never been the subject of fiction. "Discontent, conflict, waste, sorrow and fear" were its inevitable subjects. It is my hope and _____ that our _____ deal with _____

William Reed's handwritten notes are treasured by colleagues, friends and patients who receive them, and he keeps folders full of those that were sent to him.

Left – After his own heart surgery, Dr. Reed created the Cardiac Patient Liaison nursing position at St. Luke's and KU's heart program.

Below – Bill Reed chats with visitors at the Dr. William A. and Mary J. Reed Cardiovascular Surgery Center.

"Develop your ability to take in what others are trying to tell you; the best doctors who are most loved by their patients are good listeners."

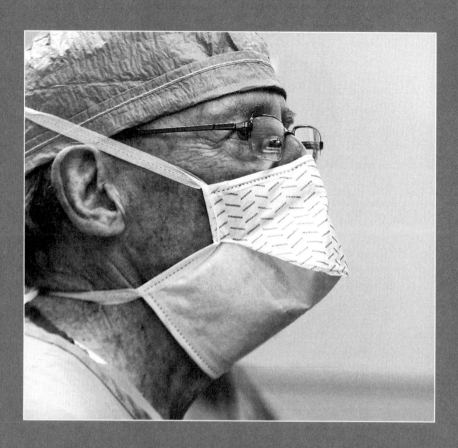

William Reed, MD, observes in the operating room in 2014.

CHAPTER 11

Servant Leader

The only wisdom we can hope to acquire

is the wisdom of humility: humility is endless.

~ T.S. Eliot, East Coker

When a lot is at stake, there is no way to describe what it's really like to be the person who's in charge. You can show confidence and even feel utterly in control while experiencing the humility and fragility that goes with that. Even when you give everything there is to give, and everyone is doing the very best he or she can, the patient can still die, the research proves fruitless, the horse breaks its neck, the vision goes unrealized, or the goal remains beyond your reach. Everyone involved feels the loss, but when you are the captain of the ship, you're going down with it. The trick is not to stay down. As Nelson Mandela said, "I would not and could not give myself up to despair. Judge me by how many times I fell down and got back up again."

It almost helps that I started at the bottom. If my humble origins gave me a view of life at the ground level, or even lower, well, it wasn't a bad place to be when considering how to build something strong from the ground up. It's an asset to know from experience how to navigate out of a tough spot, especially when others are aboard. One learns early on that very little can be accomplished by working alone. You need people . . . their energy radiating to you and making things happen that you wouldn't have felt possible. That's an energy source I can tap into to find the strength to get back up again, but if I haven't opened myself up to what others can give me, I'm missing out. So I strive to be a leader who openly encourages that giving.

If you're sending clear signals that everyone's input—from the meek to the exalted—is important to the process, and then actually reflect it in what you're creating together, you'll get the best outcome. Getting everyone's input sends them the message that you value what they can contribute, and this is how to invest each person in the endeavor. People respond when they're valued. I believe this passionately. Whenever I've been called upon to take a leadership role, my approach has always been to listen deeply and genuinely, then facilitate and support.

> *He was a man who came from sparse beginnings and he's never forgotten that. It makes him so sensitive to his patients and everyone else he encounters. You don't often see that in physicians. We expect our doctors to be really confident and assured, which Dr. Reed has along with this great humility of his. If he is in a meeting, he sits and listens to what everyone else has to say, then he shares his own wisdom. Everyone there might have strong opinions, and that might be true for Dr. Reed, too, but he takes in what others have said. I've seen him change his point of view on an issue after listening to others' points of view. For example, I had a different opinion of the placement of cardiac rehab in the new heart center at KU. He asked me in a sincere manner to explain my point, so I did. He was making sure we had what we needed to do our jobs properly. He wanted to know what that would look like from a nurse's point of view. His response was "that's all I needed to know." He shifted his position on it and it worked out fine.*

> *~ Pat Twenter, RN*

My definition of leadership is to help people do something together they couldn't accomplish alone. Leadership is not about being out front for any sort of ego-reinforcing purpose. It's not about me; it's about us . . . the team. How can I help you achieve what we're going to do together? An effective leader is one who encourages and enables people to do their best. This puts the leader in the role of service . . . giving support as needed to achieve the goals we've established together or must deliver on for someone else. It's about involving people, not just informing them. And it's about what you and I have done to be prepared for the challenge—the hard work each of us puts into being the best version of ourselves so we can be a real asset to a team.

> *He was so ahead of his time. We talk about "team medicine" now, but back in those days, it hadn't been thought of yet. Except by him—he thought of it. From the cleaning people to the equipment maintenance staff to the nurses and doctors, he went through the whole process, engaging every person for his or her input. And then he built the best heart institute in this area, if not the whole country.*
>
> *~ H. William "Bill" Barkman, MD, MSPH, formerly President of Medical Staff, KUMC Associate Professor*

One of our hospital administrators told me that he had been reading a book about the concept of servant leadership. He said, "Dr. Reed, you are the embodiment of what the author is teaching." That was one of the greatest compliments anyone has ever given me. I had to go look up the book, and learned that this approach is recognized and proven to be highly effective.

> *"This has changed the role of manager from one who drives results and motivation from the outside in, to one who is a servant leader—one who seeks to draw out, inspire and develop the best and highest within people from the inside out. The leader does this by engaging the entire team or organization in a process that creates a shared vision, which*

inspires each person to stretch and reach deeper within him or herself, and to use everyone's talents in whatever way is necessary to independently and interdependently achieve the shared vision."

~ *Robert K. Greenleaf, author,* **Servant Leadership**

Leadership is about what we can do together . . . finding and nurturing the best part of each person's ability; helping a person realize what he or she brings as an individual and how that fits into the collaboration of a team. My aspiration and inclination has always been towards that kind of leadership—servant leadership. It's embodied by one who . . .

1) Values diverse opinions

2) Cultivates a culture of trust

3) Develops other leaders

4) Helps people with issues

5) Encourages full participation

6) Sells instead of tells

7) Thanks you, not me

8) Thinks long term

9) Acts with humility

These are the signposts for success and satisfaction. I did not organize these factors in any order during my career but looking back, I have found each factor to be of critical importance—especially in building a cardiac treatment and care program.

As a leader, you don't want to suppress a different opinion, so I've found it helpful to listen carefully and not share my thoughts until everyone else has had a chance to express themselves. In doing so, I keep myself open to the possibility of changing my mind given more of the facts could result in a better decision. I'm watching carefully, too. Eye contact is very important, and my body language—not crossing my arms over my chest or carrying a posture that makes me look closed to the conversation. I'm watching to see if others are listening or diddling with their cell phones. I might ask a question directly to someone who seems reluctant to participate in an open discussion. In a large meeting where one or two persons are dominating the conversation, I try to tactfully moderate. I'll find a spot where I can step into the monologue and redirect with a question about the issue to someone we haven't heard from yet. My style is not unique, but I offer it as validation of those tactics that have proven again and again to be effective.

Leaders have to get input from others, especially honest input, in order to shepherd the group towards its best work. In medicine, the stakes are so high—life and death—so having everyone doing their best work is critical. The most important leadership effort I can make is to inspire everyone to do his or her best so their contribution fits the right way—like a puzzle. That's what it takes to complete the picture, and that's how we can do the best job for the patient.

> *He is just a wonderful person to be around, so sophisticated and brilliant. He understands what it takes to bring a team together.*
>
> ~ *Irene Thompson (formerly Irene Cumming, President and CEO, KUMC) University Health Consortium President*

I can help in different ways nowadays. I can say and do things I couldn't when I was in practice, and I can share input that has been informed by decades of experience. It's a wonderful feeling when you realize you're reaching out and offering something that can demonstrably help people. I can be effective and feel positive about the contributions I make at church, but at the hospital the advantage is—right or wrong, deserved or not—that people listen more carefully. I made a fairly unpopular statement in a committee that "just because it's legal doesn't make it right" and got a note later from someone there who thanked me for doing that. It was a point he'd been trying to make without success.

In the course of my work, I have sometimes had to bring my own concerns or those of the group forward when I felt I was in a position to do so for the right reasons—to speak truth to power. Some of those opportunities have presented themselves over the years in the legislative process. I'm not a gregarious person, so anytime I've had to fulfill a function of this sort, it has been an effort to make myself stand in the spotlight. But it's is the kind of thing a leader has to do, so I've done the best I could with that charge. In 2009, I was nominated by Senator Steve Morris, who was President of the Kansas Senate then, to serve on the Kansas Health Policy Authority. However reticent I am to be on stage, I do feel compelled to speak for those who need representation. Over the years, I've seen so many people struggle to overcome the challenges they face from poverty or disease . . . often unsuccessfully. As I scc it, any one of us in a position to relieve that should feel the responsibility to at least try.

The interesting thing is that he went on to do things I'd never believe . . . he's quite a verbally convincing statesman. Bill gets in and understands all those issues and what's behind them in the Kansas Legislature. I'd have never predicted that was something he could do. His career was in the OR where his hands spoke for him; he never spent any time talking. But there he was at the capital, years later. He's got a new skillset and he's very effective with it, but he never brags on it. Bill's one of those people . . . his least favorite topic is himself.

~ Charles Porter, MD

I've worked behind the scenes with him on some of these issues with the Kansas legislature. Bill was no longer practicing medicine but clearly involved in the program and its level of quality since we have had national recognition for a number of years now. Over the years we've become friends working together on a legislative agenda. Bill is easy to work with. He is a superb colleague—knowledgeable, respectful, always does his homework, he's always prepared.

Legislators aren't used to having a physician come down to the capital and talk to them directly. While he might be a man of few words, Bill Reed gets the critical points across effectively. He was one of few people who actually practiced medicine and could bring that dimension, so he was appointed to the Kansas Health Policy Authority. He went to hearings and was well received. His mannerisms are professional but non-intimidating. He's a multidimensional guy. Because of the diversity of his background—his horse racing at the national recognition level—people ask him about the horses without realizing who he is to the field of medicine. This allows him to interact with so many different kinds of people. He knows so many different disciplines and that gives him the ability to talk to so many people.

~ H. William "Bill" Barkman, MD, MSPH, formerly President of Medical Staff, KUMC Associate Professor

Bill Reed doesn't feel the need to fill a room; he's comfortable in his own skin. He doesn't need the limelight, and is happy to be engaged in one-on-one conversations with anyone about the weather or the meaning of life.

~ Reverend Edward Thompson

*Name any major figure in heart surgery—DeBakey, Cooley—
giants in the field but their greatness was all about them.
That's not a very long lasting model. Once that person flames
out, you've got nothing left. Dr. Reed is a very unique person
in that way. His humility is singular . . . it's about more than
him. The focus is always on getting what's best for the patients
. . . what's best for the whole team. His strongest assets are his
selflessness and ability to bring people together to accomplish
excellence. Even the money he's donated—he isn't looking for
awards or kudos—he never has. Bill Reed gets his satisfaction
from knowing that he's done something good for people.*

~ Jeffrey Kramer, MD

$\mathcal{T}$he greatest reward in life is helping someone. We must
understand what a privilege it is, and to be true to that trust. For me,
it has meant recognizing and acknowledging that being of service is
what I have to do with my life.

*As compared to other medical leaders, I'd be hard pressed
to find another who embodies servant leadership the way
Bill Reed does. He approaches things from a patient-first
perspective, always looking for how we can better meet the
needs of the patient. Bill was a rock star as a lobbyist. You get
this guy with his reputation in a white coat, his wisdom and
relevancy . . . he commands attention. He had the legislators
lined up.*

*~ Bob Page, President and CEO,
The University of Kansas Hospital*

Plants are like people

Stamen to pistil
So beautiful
in early bloom
Some grow briefly
    bright and
quickly done
Some mature slowly
branching through
    the cycles of life
Some are strong
    Surviving deeply
    withering winters
Some tendershoots need
    nurturing words
    and nursing
Some reach, yearning
    for enough Light
    to dim despair
Some bring us
    joy and celebrations
a baby's breath at birth or
poppies dark red as a door

~ William Reed

Having been a "nobody" as a child, I feel keenly aware of the necessity to make everyone with whom I work and live know that they have value . . . not only to me but to life. While there were those who looked at me as a child and saw nothing of significance—and certainly a superficial view didn't contradict that—I speak from personal experience when I say that kindness and personal attention can make all the difference for any individual. If living in poverty and privation taught me that nobody is a nobody, then I would tell you my childhood was worth suffering because it shaped my view of humanity.

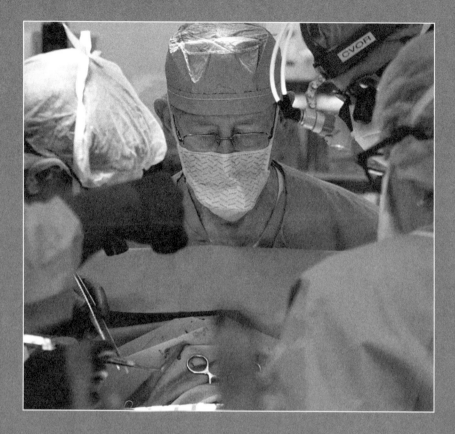

"I hope that it takes hold of you—that you have both the passion
as well as an innate sense of responsibility to do this work. This is a calling."
~ William Reed, MD

CHAPTER 12

The Legacy

It's one of the most beautiful compensations of this life

that no man can sincerely try to help another

without helping himself.

~ *Ralph Waldo Emerson*

The circumstances of my youth made me very aware that for many of us the opportunity for success may require a boost from someone along the way. Any one of us who has ever benefitted from someone else's genuine kindness recognizes the sense of worth that conveys, and the obligation to be worthy. Everything I have accomplished has been made possible by such grace. It's a gift I'm keenly aware of, and the magnitude of it makes me speechless at times. When one is without words, it moves you to do something . . . to give something back. Every time I've been given an opportunity to do so—to provide someone else with a boost—I've looked at it as a means to pay it back or even forward. It's the best way I know to express my own gratitude for the blessings of my life. I am certain that the more I've given, the more I have received. Beyond that, I will let the others speak to the notion of my legacy. For me, whatever good I've been able to do has been "the most beautiful compensation of this life."

> *Once when we were living out at Stonecrest Farm while waiting to move into our new house, there was a man in a truck, a plumber, driving around trying to find the house. I asked if I could help him, he seemed lost. He asked if Dr. Reed lived here. I said yes, do you want me to find him? He said no, then he just got calm and looked around . . . he just was paying his respects because Dr. Reed had saved his life.*
>
> ~ *Reverend Clayton Smith*

> *Dr. Reed's legacy is as the man behind the rebirth of cardiovascular disease at KU. Tremendous accolades as practitioner and the commitment he and Mary have given to this effort.*
>
> *Today he's still very active, moving forward in the face of all the changes in terms of the Affordable Care Act and Medicare funding. With the cost of devices and care for cardiovascular health today, how will we manage in the face of financial constraints? I just don't think many of us know, but he's on it. Bill's got the depth and breadth and vision and concern. He's still got it. He's a unique package.*
>
> ~ *H. William "Bill" Barkman, MD, MSPH,*
> *formerly President of Medical Staff, KUMC Associate Professor*

> *Reed's legacy is changing the perception of KUMC from bottom of the heap to a real bastion of excellence.*
>
> ~ *Representative Steve Morris,*
> *Kansas State Legislature*

Giving and Growing

I found a time

in my life

when I had little to give

Reaching out to find a

route to a new life

What I discovered, what

I learned, how I changed

Helping God heal the sick

was a great privilege

a blessing.

It opened my heart to

share with others

The material things

seemed to grow with

the giving and so did I

~ William Reed

Dr. Reed is always a professional . . . whether you agree or disagree with him, he is the consummate professional. He's a man of few words, but they're powerful words. He's done a lot of things for people and wants no recognition. He does it because he believes it's the right thing to do. He will have multiple legacies, one of which will be the creation of a world class cardiovascular program. To go from a department that barely existed to the US News & World Report's Top 50 and stay there for seven years in a row and counting—remarkable. I think it's sustainable for many years into the future. As an individual, his legacy is even bigger. It's about him as a human being, his gracious, humble and generous spirit.

*~ Tammy Peterman, Executive Vice President,
COO & CNO, KUMC*

I always think of Dr. Reed as having a couple careers. He's probably ready to launch his third no doubt. Back in 2007, we had some significant battles in the Kansas legislature. We always called him our secret weapon. You can bring a lot of people up to testify and influence the thinking at the capital, but Dr. Reed was in a very unique position indeed. He's very serious, but warmhearted with an incredible wit. He commands respect for what he's done, and legislators appreciate hearing from someone with his credentials as a physician. There was an immediate trust. He established some critically important relationships that were extremely helpful to us in our efforts to support the best healthcare for citizens of our state.

Plus, Bill Reed doesn't need or want anything from anyone. All he wants is to see KU's heart program and the hospital to be successful. When people sense and know that, you're so much more effective in whatever you do. Certainly, KUMC is bigger than the body of work he's done, but Dr. Reed and Dr. Kindred brought their groups over here and that was, without a doubt, the turnaround of this hospital.

*~ Representative Kathy Wolf Moore,
Kansas State Legislature*

Bill Reed will be remembered as one of the best heart surgeons ever. He singlehandedly developed the heart program at St. Luke's. It's now a leading cardiac center in the nation. Wherever he was, there'd be a fantastic heart program. Even now, he still stands as the best here at KUMC and even over the country as a whole, in my opinion.

~ Lynn Kindred, MD

He was a pioneer in thoracic surgery. He was getting outcomes no one else was having . . . he was the best at the time. He set the bar for those to follow. His caliber of operation—he was so fast, no wasted movements, no unnecessary steps—so the patient had less anesthesia and less blood loss so they just did better. Today he is still a forward thinker. He knows what's going on. So I worked alongside him until he quit in 2003. He said, "It's best to leave when nobody is telling you to go . . . before your skills falter." So he quit operating on his own terms. He left at the top of his game.

~ Elaine Russell, RN

For all his accomplishments, he's just so humble and he's got all this common sense. He still does critical thinking on health policy all the way down to the level of care.

~ Lynn Kindred, MD

Bill was the busiest surgeon in Kansas City in his heyday. He's sort of a renaissance man. Once minute he's talking surgery, the next he's quoting poetry. He's very thoughtful . . . interested in and knows about so many things.

~ Jeffrey Kramer, MD

Bill Reed is the American Dream personified. He has never bragged on his success, and he's never forgotten his humble beginnings. Whether he realizes it or not, he takes that mannerism with him wherever he goes. It's what people respond to from all walks of life.

~ State Representative Kathy Wolf Moore,
Kansas State Legislature

A man in his late eighties came through on a tour of our Heart Institute. About forty years earlier, Reed had operated on his daughter when she was little and saved her life. This old fellow had tears in his eyes as he talked about it. He was still so grateful.

~ Lynn Kindred, MD

I have to say that Mary deserves so much credit. She majors in the heart, and he majors in the head. She brings the emotional gifts and he brings the intellectual gifts. It's a pretty strong combination. What a dynamic duo these two people are. I think Bill and Mary both have the beautiful gift from God to see the best in people in all situations. Yet they don't believe there is anything special about them. Their humility is genuine.

~ Reverend Clayton Smith

Bill Reed takes a great deal of time to handwrite notes with from-the-heart comments. They're treasures. He wrote to me when my father died. A deep thought, nothing superficial, but from the heart and meaningful.

~ Tammy Peterman, Executive Vice President, COO & CNO, KUMC

I think Mary shares in his legacy. The fact is that if Bill or Mary could do anything to make somebody's life better, they would. Behind every great man is a great woman, and so many things that Mary does actually improve his reputation. For instance, she is totally in charge of the horse camp we do here at Stonecrest Farm each year. She gives the inner-city kids who come out these gift bags and snacks. They learn about horses and the sport of horse racing responsibly. That's all Mary. In fact, Mary Reed deserves the lion's share of the credit for making the Kansas City Mounted Patrol viable. She created a foundation to raise money and keep them funded. She believes in the power of horses to calm people down, and to do things cops can't do on their own. She's right about that. She's the same way with donating to vet clinics so care can be given to animals that need medical help or to be put down and there's no one to pay. Once I had a dog that needed surgery that was going to cost $2500. I've got four kids, so I just couldn't rationalize it. Mary called me and asked if she could cover the cost for my dog's surgery. So that's what happened. You know how many times she's held that over my head? Zero. Not once.

My brother got killed in a motorcycle wreck in 2010. It happened on a Wednesday night. I had to run back and forth from Kansas City to Lincoln, Nebraska, during that time. The Reeds were so understanding; Dr. Reed came over to the barn one day and just handed me some cash . . . said he wanted to make sure I was ok, that he knew all the trips were a financial hit. I was struggling with losing my brother and best friend, and he just took the financial strain away without a question. No commentary or mention of a loan, he just handed me enough money to take that stress off my shoulders. That's the kind of guy Dr. Reed is.

~ Garrett Smith, Stonecrest Farm trainer

He was a second father to me when mine passed away. He backed me up and was right there with me same as my father was. If I'd needed to go to him for advice, or even now if I needed to, I know he'd be there.

~ Henry Pearley, RN

Losing my son Ted was tough, and Bill was there for me. Ted's motto was "practice excellence." I always think, if anybody in this world could be said to live by that slogan, it would be Bill Reed. Everything he did, he practiced excellence.

~ Bill Hamaker, MD

I volunteered as an orderly when I was fifteen at St. Luke's. We brought things to the lab, took patients in wheelchairs or gurneys to X-ray, and ran errands. The first summer I was there, I remember being surprised that when people found out I was Jeff Reed, son of the Dr. Reed, they'd always stop me to talk. There were two women who worked in the X-ray area who looked at my name tag and asked, "Are you related to Dr. Reed?" Yes, I'm his son, I said, then I braced myself for whatever was going to happen next. They said, "Do you know how great a man your dad is!?" I said no, why? They told me Dad treated them like they were the most important people in the hospital. I'd hear the same thing from the janitors in the ER. Everyone went out of his or her way to tell me how great my dad was. Once a nurse just blurted out, "Your dad is fantastic." They'd just come out of the woodwork with comments like that. What I learned from that was how you treat other people has a huge impact on how they feel about themselves. No matter who you are, no matter where you go, you always treat everybody like they're the most important people who exist. That's been a life lesson I've learned directly and indirectly from my dad.

~ Jeff Reed

Two generations later, nobody remembers who you are, but every medical student and doctor in practice ought to know Bill Reed. He is, without question, among the best and the brightest. Bill Reed made more contributions to cardiothoracic medicine than anyone around here, then to establish that heart center. It'll be there forever. His is a long-lasting legacy. He was the man.

~ Bill Hamaker, MD

I want to stress Bill's humanity . . . not just his surgical skill but his capacity to care for human consciousness. He is so much more than a heart surgeon, he is a holistic healer. He understands the "privilege" part of being a doctor . . . that you must have love, as Paracelsus once said, to become a real physician. Bill is able to give that love as well as his cardiovascular expertise to his patients.

~ Jo Jeanne Callaway, MD

William Reed at Stonecrest Farm, 2013

CHAPTER 13

Poet and Philosopher

The heart has its reasons of which reason knows nothing.

~ Blaise Pascal

A legacy is a very public thing, so I hope to leave a good one. Yet, each of us has three lives: a public life, a private life, and a secret life, as Irish author Frank Delaney puts it. Any man writing the story of his own life must decide which version of it he'll share. His decision may change from chapter to chapter, or even sentence to sentence. Sometimes between the noun and the verb it changes. Then the story takes on a life of its own and debates its expression heatedly. It insists on honest disclosure while dancing behind seven veils of perspective.

Let those who think I have said too little and those who think
I have said too much, forgive me, and let those who think
I have said just enough thank God with me.

~ St. Augustine

The truth is that we are not just happening to ourselves. There are parts of my story that belong to others, so I have not shared anything but my own perspective except where others are quoted. I have tried to keep any secrets that don't belong solely to me. Yet there is the secret that wants to be known. It becomes a rock in the shoe . . . it cannot be ignored. In truth, it is much more a mystery than a secret: how does a man who has had all these blessings dare to question his existence? I suppose I am telling my story for the same reason I used to make a clay model of a complicated heart abnormality—so I could demonstrate how I fixed it, if indeed I did. Now I share how I solved the mystery of myself . . . if indeed I have.

Science and technology cannot answer all the questions I've pondered. Religion hasn't satisfied my doubts, but I feel compelled to believe in God even as I question what God is. Oxford theologian Keith Ward wrote, ". . . belief in God might not be founded on reason, as though it is a hypothesis to explain why the universe is the way it is. But reason has to get to work on those human experiences that give rise to belief in God." That articulates so well what it means to question existence—to ask the big questions. What is the point of pain and suffering? What is love if not the hope of being loved, and isn't that a selfish motivation in the end? What happens after that last breath?

Bill Reed asks the hardest questions . . . he's very good at doubt.

~ Reverend Edward Thompson

The way I've approached the mystery is to take pieces of reality and put them together to see if they work. Now I'm at the point where I can see which pieces are real and which are not. Health issues, end of life anxieties, trying to figure all this out—is there anything good that can come of putting it all out there? After a lifetime spent holding someone's heart in my hand, I feel absurd wearing my own on my sleeve. Still, it is an offering I'm willing to make—after a lifetime of walking, I'll shine some light on the shadow that's followed me around on my journey. As Carl Jung said, "The shadow is the least desirable aspect of one's personality." Mine is always pressing the point of something unknown. It fills me with the ache of Thoreau's "quiet desperation," even as I step solidly through the grace of my own life, completely humbled by the beauty and blessedness of it.

Ah, when to the heart of man

was it ever less than a treason

to go with the drift of things

to yield with a grace to reason,

and bow and accept the end

of a love or a season?

~ *Robert Frost, in Reluctance*

My answers are incomplete, and they may not work for others any more than their conclusions could work for me. If I just admit that approaching the end of life is a frightening, confusing chaos—do all the realities my life has stood for then lose their meaning? Wouldn't it be wrong to put that on anybody else? Mary would say that I've experienced more divinely-driven events than anyone could count. How could I not believe? Yet the truth is that my insides won't let me take that as a solid reality. I still have my doubts . . . but I also have hope.

To choose doubt as a philosophy of life
is akin to choosing immobility as a means of transportation.

~ *Yann Martel, **Life of Pi***

Even with the achievements of my life, there is still a part of me that feels very much the way I did when I was a little boy . . . detached and alone. I surround myself with books full of my closest friends. I'm grateful that the poets and philosophers wrote about their secrets and darkness, so maybe someone will find consolation in my doing so. Most of the deepest conversations I have had have been an internal dialogue with the great writers and thinkers who have struggled with the same issues as I. We understand each other. We wring our hands together . . . hold them up to the heavens like so many trees.

If the first poets I knew were trees, then the ones who followed were real men and women who made a wondrous forest with their words. I "keep adding . . . keep walking" for answers, as St. Augustine said, until I get there. I feel at home in this space, an old pine that provides shelter year-round for those who need it. I ponder the "luminous pause between two great mysteries," as Carl Jung put it.

> *I can only make this one bold statement of faith,*
> *I absolutely believe in something . . .*
> *even if I don't know what it is.*
>
> ~ William Reed

Mary has been given the gift of unquestioning faith, so has my son Jeff, but I have not. I envy them theirs. Faith is a gift and sometimes it isn't there for me. I think my other boys, Bryan and Martin, could relate to that, but it's not something we discuss.

My platelet count is low . . . it can convert to leukemia, I'm aware of this. So I've had some health problems although I feel fine. This experience just made my feelings more vivid. It has made me aware of my vulnerability. My main concern now is Mary. What would her life be like if I wasn't here? Such thoughts don't take me to any good place.

We have had a strong, loving relationship, but not a perfect one. We've both made compromises or resigned ourselves to realities we couldn't change. For the first seven years of our marriage, Mary's focus was entirely on me. Frankly, she spoiled me rotten. After the children arrived, her attention shifted to our sons, which was where it needed to be; I understood that. But this left me feeling a new kind of loneliness. In the self-imposed exile I made over our religious differences, I felt even more isolated. It was important to me that Mary's strong faith not be questioned or shaken by my lack of belief, so I kept that part of me—the part that sought for answers I didn't have—quiet, unknown for the most part. This created a distance between us—a place we couldn't dwell together. We both felt it, and suffered over this since spirituality is so important to both of us. This quiet part of who I am has remained largely unknown right in the midst of my own family. In spite of this, Mary and I have been together for over sixty years, so I guess we've figured one another out and accepted who we are in the end. We haven't given up on each other.

Sometimes I think about who's going to die first, how terrible for the other one. I worry that Mary would have an inability to cope with that, but I could be wrong. She is no doubt stronger than I give her credit for. I know she has tremendous strength in her own right. She's had to put up with a lot being married to me. My tendency towards the "brown study" of life has surely left her lonely as well.

> *He's so protective of Mary in her certainty of faith. He protects it. He doesn't want to disturb it like a house of cards you couldn't pull a single one from . . . he doesn't have that stack. For Bill Reed, it's the now, not the hereafter. He allows himself the wonder and mystery without certainty. His faith isn't scheme and doctrines or a set of propositions that would freeze life in a vacuum. His medical career and life experience has shown him more than that.*
>
> *~ Reverend Edward Thompson*

etirement prompted an internal milieu. Yes, I made a plan and I'm living it fully, I hope. Not surprisingly, it involves horses and hospitals. Yes, I still go into the office and serve on various committees. I'm the Chair of the Department of Cardiovascular Diseases at KUMC, and Chairman of the Quality Assurance Committee within that department. We're facing an unprecedented challenge to provide affordable, quality medical care in the face of staggering costs, not only at KUMC but on the national scale. That discussion draws me, and the field of medicine still fascinates me. I want to see where we'll go next. I don't ever want to feel that I have nothing left to contribute because that really is the end.

> *Dad recognizes it's a new day for him—that there is still an opportunity to make a difference. He is in a position where he can voice his opinion in a new way. He's free to speak his mind now, and what's on his mind is valuable to the hospital and to the field. He can use his position and perspective to do things the younger doctors can't. He still enjoys the challenge.*
>
> *~ Jeff Reed*

I think about the author Ross Lockridge who wrote Raintree County. He lived in a two room apartment with his wife and two kids while he was writing the book, and after it was published, he committed suicide. Something about that strikes me as akin to a postpartum depression or maybe the sense that one's life mission is done and there is nothing left to live for, yet you're still alive. It's a dangerous period of time.

I have never seriously thought about suicide, I want to stay alive. In 2003, I was suspected of having myelodysplastic syndrome, a disease that destroys bone marrow. At first we thought that it would be fatal. I was writing notes to leave for my kids and Mary, which prompted a lot of contemplation. What had I lived for, and how does one prepare to die? I realized it's not the fear of dying, which is just a moment in time, but the suffering that comes from fear. And fear comes from the unknown. Rationally, death happens to everybody, that's the way it is. What happens on the other side of that is unknown in any verifiable way.

I find myself lacking the vocabulary to explain "something even non-believers can believe in," as Bacharach put it. People put names on things, they label them, but how do you name God? Even if I don't know for sure what it is, it feels real . . . it becomes a matter of attaching a label to a feeling. When my brother Jay was traveling with a quartet singing gospel, he once complimented a piano player at a church where they performed. She was just wonderful and joyful in her playing, and her response was, "That's the Jesus in me." Although she expressed it differently than I would, I think I agree with her—some things are given to us as a gift from God. Of course, then a person like me goes on to ask if life is a gift from God, why then is it taken back? Is it any wonder I envy Mary and Jeff their comfortable foundation in faith?

Almost every morning I go to the chapel to think. I try hard to think about joyful things, and find it easy to be grateful for the many blessings of my life. Still, sometimes I have to work very hard at joy. I do know this—it is important and necessary to work at joy if you are the kind of person who isn't imbued with that outlook. It is a worthy endeavor and it pays off. Optimism is a life skill that can be honed with practice. We can consciously choose to be positive or negative, and that view will create the next set of circumstances accordingly. Or perhaps the circumstances choose us and this is also how God works.

Whatever shadows are there only serve to emphasize the light, and it's just not that helpful for any of us to dwell on them. Just because you could think a guy who left his wife and kids and ran to the Bahamas is a cretin doesn't make him so. You don't know why he made that choice, so you can't judge. Nor can I judge the woman who is having an abortion, even though I have always found it ironic that I could be struggling to save someone's life in one OR while a brand new life is being intentionally ended in another OR. But it is not for me to pass judgment, so I don't.

True sacrifice is the offering of self so God can realize the power of the activity in and through your life. God is one who commands love, who forgives our inability to love, who places the Divine loss within us and who will insure that love is then stronger than death. God's love is illimitable. Worshipers should seek to feel and know the pain and happiness of all creatures which will inevitably lead to their seeking to alleviate pain and rejoice in the many forms of happiness. It will lead to lives of true compassion and shared joy.

~ Keith Ward, PhD, God: A Guide for the Perplexed

If I had to summarize a gift from each of them, it would be my dad's humility and respect for everyone equally. From my mom, I got the ability to see something positive in everything that happens. Through the conflicts in her life and mine, just everyday conflicts, she always looks at the bright side. My mom taught me that no matter how bad it gets, there's a reason for it and something to learn from it.

~ Jeff Reed

I invited Dr. Reed to speak to our patient support group on the history of cardiac medicine. He shared a personal story of his own heart surgery in 1985. You could have heard a pin drop. He said, "I've been a patient myself," not just this high-powered surgeon. He was willing to talk about the impact of spirituality on heart surgery—not a topic you'd expect to hear from a surgeon. One of the patients asked, "I was wondering if surgeons stop and pray?" Dr. Reed replied, "Always."

~ Pat Twenter, RN

Doors

Time was when by thrust
to open doors
To see what lay behind
The unexplored to find
the challenges and leap
into the rush of feeling
Grasping the emotion of
Reaching out and onward
Into what might have remained
A mystery for all time
To embrace the intensity
Of this new spirit
that takes a piece
of who I am
and where you are left is now
a final resting place of aloneness
Am I afraid to
Be alone?
Yet we all must make that
journey on our own
Until behind that last door
Will I find those
who have gone before?
In joy and music and poetry
where I will be alone – no more?

~ William Reed

I understand the practical reality of the lifespan. We are told that we're put here for a reason. In order for a life to have meaning, it must have worth. How you measure worth is primarily how you treat other people. So the meaning must derive from how much you have given of yourself to others, I think. If you didn't contribute anything, if you were a manipulator and taker all your life, then what did your life stand for? What did it mean? What possible reason could you have been alive? Don't we all need to answer that for ourselves before we die? Every man dies alone with his God. If that god is politics or money or addiction or love or even religion—that is the last face you'll see. It's going into the ground with you so it had better be worth it.

> *In 1981, I went out to a conference in Kansas City and I got to stay with Uncle Bill and Aunt Mary. That was the first time I got to spend time with him as an adult and explore the issues of faith with him. His faith was much more important to him than his financial rewards.*
>
> *~ Greg Reed, nephew*

Living in harmony with your values, exemplary in every way you could possibly be, a person should experience the peace that surpasses all understanding. For a while my spirit rests easy with that explanation, until my pervasive discontent resurfaces . . . a new question emerges. It's as if I haven't even asked the right question yet. Actually, my bigger fear is that I'll stop asking questions.

Why couldn't I have just as easily been born a horse and be spared all this thinking?

> *Where had I heard this wind before*
> *Change like this to a deeper roar?*
> *What would it take my standing there for,*
> *Holding open a restive door,*

Looking down hill to a frothy shore?
Summer was past and the day was past.
Sombre clouds in the west were massed.
Out on the porch's sagging floor,
Leaves got up in a coil and hissed,
Blindly struck at my knee and missed.
Something sinister in the tone
Told me my secret must be known:
Word I was in the house alone
Somehow must have gotten abroad,
Word I was in my life alone,
Word I had no one left but God.

~ Robert Frost, Bereft

Being a man who sees tree poets, I also hear existential anthems in a pop song. "What's it all about, Alfie? Is it just for the moment we live?" Reflection comes gently or in a fever dream. Regardless, I try to make myself look at all this with acceptance and grace. It is not a new thing for me to ponder the great mysteries, but to ask "is that all there is?" at my age sounds like I have given up on the answer. I haven't, nor will I stop turning these rocks over to see what's underneath all my doubts and fears because I don't want the answer to give up on me.

> *He's come to openness about expressing doubt . . . a dynamic doubt that helps lead us to identify the right questions, not the despairing doubt that drives us to fear or anxiety. Bill Reed doesn't allow his fear to grow in his doubt. He allows his faith to grow in his doubt. That's a sign of maturity. His strong moral framework drives him to seek something of greater significance.*
>
> *~ Reverend Clayton Smith*

I guess that's part of the dilemma now. How do I wrap it up? That's what's causing the trouble with me now, I can't grasp certain realities. They're changing. And what's real to me isn't a reality to a lot of other people I see people in church on Sunday. All the lonely people—where do they all come from? All the smiling faces at church . . . can they all be so happy? And if they are, I don't want to dissuade them; I don't want to disturb that reality. What do they know that I don't? Were they born with a gift of faith? If so, why wasn't I?

What if some of us have the same doubts and fears and we've all been hiding behind our smiles? What if we dared to tell the truth to each other . . . assuming we could even admit it to ourselves?

> *I think Bill's whole life has been St. Augustine's walking. The next encounter, the next search for another answer or way of doing something . . . whether it's in the human body for the betterment of human life, Bill Reed is constantly doing that.*
>
> *Bill and I have connected because I am this religious authority figure who has given him permission—not that it is mine to give—to go deeper into fear. I've pushed him to explore the emptiness . . . the open space. Not a vacuum or deep hole, but I try to encourage him to become comfortable in the deep cloud of unknowing. I want to affirm that it is ok not to have structure. What we believe doesn't have to be a set of propositions. He asks these deep questions of himself. He goes inward to search . . . a hermit soul who is happy in the search and energized by the mystery. Bill's heart and mind are restless. I don't think he has a sense of inner peace. We talk about this; I can relate to it.*
>
> *~ Reverend Edward Thompson*

Walking for Answers

How do you know
Where you are going
until you discover
why you are going?

How do you share
the aloneness
without spreading loneliness?

How do you find
the right answers
until you ask the right questions?

How do you find
your own way
until you discover the right path?

How do you share
the love you feel
unless you have been loved?

How do you find God
while you are still
in the wilderness?

~ William Reed, 2013

$\mathcal{A}$s a boy, I'd wake up in the middle of the night and realize that one day I would die. I don't believe in fire and brimstone with a tailed devil wielding a pitchfork, but I can't help but think there are moments in everyone's life when they reflect on the fact that they won't exist in the form they know now. Who can truly know what comes after this? Death is a celebration according to Jeff. For me, I have a problem with the notion of angels playing harps in clouds. I don't think seeing streets of gold and grandma again is going to happen. That's what I really believe. I think you live forever if there are those who will carry a memory of you, but beyond that I don't know what the afterlife is. It's hard to find peace when you struggle with some concept of an alternative to oblivion that isn't just "pablum for the fearful." When my sister was critically ill with pulmonary disease, she told me she saw an entity in the corner of the hospital room. I don't disbelieve her, but I don't think I'll see one myself.

When you consider the energy it takes to become who we are, said the philosopher Robertson Davies, it's absurd to think there is nothing behind all this. Just because we can't prove something doesn't mean it doesn't exist. It takes some imagination. If you look at the Bible, it's filled with symbolic meaning. Of course, a lot of people read it literally, but for me it's more helpful to consider its meaning on a metaphorical level. Like music, however different it might have sounded two thousand years ago, it still does what music does to our souls. Whatever reaches us . . . teaches, expands and inspires us is a timeless, mythic and metaphysical reality that can't always be expressed in literal terms. In fact, the effort to understand it at the local-literal level usually negates the very essence of this feeling. Our efforts to confine it to language restrict it. Music, poetry, and the natural world consist of the energy it takes to become who we are. There are times when such things touch me so deeply that I do feel I am in the presence of angels.

Dad has always been drawn to poetry. It's more of a personal liking of his that is not particularly shared by the rest of us to *the same extent, although Martin may have something to say on that. I believe that we both enjoyed Cormac McCarthy's **The Road** despite our different views on its interpretation. And, of course, we have both been drawn to **A River Runs Through It** for the obvious reason that it portrays fly fishing as meditative and an integral part of life . . . a gift given from a father to his sons.*

~ Bryan Reed

*I*f Pascal is right—the search itself is God—then here is what I have found God to be: another, more Divine explanation for the seeming randomness of life's beauty and synchronicity. It's impossible to say that the things that happened in my life were just random. There is clearly some kind of higher power, and God is a good word for it, so I call it God.

I know that I cannot relate to a God who brings pain. Yet I have seen people use the pain they have experienced to accomplish great growth. In **The Problem of Pain**, C.S. Lewis says that it's possible to grow through suffering. I think pain and suffering can be ennobling. They are the package that a certain kind of wisdom comes in, although many of us refuse to open it. But what is the point of pain and sickness when it isn't ennobling anybody—when it's just unfair, tragic and pointless? I'm convinced that suffering is an unavoidable part of life. It wouldn't have been nearly as believable to me if Jesus had skipped over to the cross. What impacted me powerfully was his question: why have you forsaken me? I know that feeling. If you are a person (or a surgeon) who has been called to stand helpless and hopeless in the presence of great pain and suffering—to open wounds literally or figuratively—then you know the process is necessary to create the possibility of healing. Yet why do some of us heal while others don't? Would God forsake any one of us? How could an all-loving God do that?

To believe is human, to doubt is divine.

~ Peter Rollins, Irish Theologian

One quiet evening in the late spring as Mary and I were finishing dinner, a terrible kind of pain broke the tranquility and brought suffering right to our door. Our trainer Garrett Smith's children had been taking a shortcut through a paddock back to their house when three year old Tenley got kicked in the face by one of the horses. Jaxson, ten years old, and Kaelee, eight, took turns carrying their baby sister, even climbing the fence with her, until they finally reached our house for help. As soon as we saw them, we called the ambulance. I took the tiny girl in my arms. She was soaked with blood and still bleeding. As we waited for the emergency crew, I checked her vitals and assessed the damage as best I could. Her nose was broken, her eyes swelling shut . . . what I couldn't see might be far more serious. I cleaned her gently, and comforted her. She was still conscious and crying. She could move her arms and legs so I knew at that point in time that neurologically she was probably ok. Her parents got there and were frantic to know what had happened—and what might happen. I have been in this moment many times with a family, but this one was so close to home with a little child to whom I've been an adopted grandfather. Yet I was also a doctor, so with a strong, calm voice I told Jaxson, Kaelee, Garrett and his wife Lynn the good signs as I noted them. Her respirations were good, her pulse was steady. I focused on the positive. The ambulance arrived and Lynn climbed in the back beside Tenley's stretcher. I could see and hear her praying with every fiber of her maternal being, then the doors closed and they rushed Tenley to the hospital.

A few weeks later, I was pulling into the reserved parking lot at work and couldn't get the gate to open. A colleague saw my dilemma, stepped right up, swiped his keycard, and the gate lifted so I could go through. After I parked, I hurried to catch up with him. Ironically, he'd been on my mind a lot. Although I rarely had any direct contact with him at work, I was aware that he'd been dealing with some difficult challenges. I was concerned for him and we talked briefly. "Well, Bill, it's really good to see you. I take it as a good sign. You've turned many tough situations into something good. Maybe that will happen to me, too," he said. I nodded because I knew this was the truth. Inwardly, I thanked God for the dead battery in my keycard. My friend needed a reminder that things often work out even when circumstances seem quite the opposite. I was that reminder. Perhaps life had chosen the two of us for that exchange.

Into my path came a little girl with a broken face and a grown man with a heavy load. In both cases, I sensed that I was needed for what I could bring literally and figuratively to the situation. Miraculously, Tenley was going to be ok—she might barely remember her brush with death in years to come. Her mother thanked me for staying calm because it helped her feel hopeful. My colleague faced a difficult transition in his life with an emerging sense of hope. And I was transfused by each exchange—reminded of the connectivity between us all . . . my sense of purpose replenished. Perhaps I needed them even more than they needed me. Two seemingly random experiences among so many, including and especially those that didn't have a happy ending . . . what part have I played in their outcomes? Were they random or was there a reason?

I believe things happen for a reason and the reasons have to do with God, but I cannot explain why. The explanation leaves logic in a knot and, "Reason offers no path to God," as Ward says. At the end of the day, you don't have to understand why you're there, but your presence at certain critical times matters significantly, and God works with that. It becomes apparent that you are the person who is needed and what you contribute to the situation is worthy—if you chose to fulfill your purpose and prepare yourself for what life would require of you.

God's power in the world is necessarily persuasive, not coercive. God acts by self-revelation. God, who is the source of our freedom, cannot coerce the world . . . God awaits our free response, constantly and with infinite patience seeking to create the best that can be gotten from each choice we make.

~ C. Robert Mesle, *Process Theology*

Whatever God is, I find it essential to engage that higher power in prayer and contemplation as I strive to fulfill my calling. If I pray—and I have before and after every surgery I've ever performed and at every important juncture of my life—does it influence the outcome? Even though I don't know the answer, prayer is still very much a part of my preparation. I'd ask God for all the guidance I could get, although I didn't imagine an old man in robes with a long white beard was listening. I did it for the centering experience of it, and because I do believe something, something hears and feels me when I pray. I feel better and stronger for having prayed, more confident and competent. I consider prayer so important to the process of healing that Mary and I donated funds for a non-denominational chapel at KUMC so there would be a sacred space dedicated entirely to prayer and deep contemplation. Deep wounds heal from the inside out . . . superficial wounds from the outside in. Healing the heart requires both, and I mean that medically and spiritually.

People of his depth can't avoid peering over the edge and looking into the darkness. When Bill Reed experiences the dark "what if's?" and perceives only chaos, the way he intuitively as well as rationally deals with that chaos is to bring order out of it. The "is that all there is?" thread in his personality and consciousness drives him to bring as much order out of chaos as he can. So he makes the world a better place, with more love given to whatever he touches, and that is ultimately a matter of deep spirituality.

~ Jo Jeanne Callaway, MD

*T*here are very few, if any, definitive answers to theological and philosophical questions, but I strive to understand the arguments. You are seeking the thing to which you want to be committed . . . you're there emotionally. You want to make the commitment to a purpose in life in order for your life to have meaning. In that process you are not a dead man at all. You're willing to fully engage in your life. At some point along the line, most people become disillusioned and give up on their commitments. They disengage. It's just too difficult to keep growing when it requires changing, and it does require changing. Change is painful, and pain is something we intuitively avoid. Then we become the guy just living for a beer on Friday . . . or whatever constitutes escape from life.

Yet every day is a new day that we have to reach out and replenish ourselves—to commit again to doing our best and highest. Living that way and committing to growth is a difficult path. My perception of what is of uppermost importance has changed as time has marched on and I've evolved. Yet what doesn't change is how right it feels to go out and help someone, to be loving and helpful . . . that is foundational. That's what drives me.

I do believe there is a greater power that shapes our destiny and guides us to find and follow our passion. We have the responsibility of choice, and it's up to us to live responsibly with those choices. I believe I am a Christian and follow the primary obligation of that faith to reach out to others with love. I have been blessed in unbelievable ways that have convinced me that I was chosen for my purpose. This leads me to believe that for each of us there will be signs showing the way through life. The more we follow them correctly, the better we get at reading them and, ultimately, reaching the destination. Then there will be another destination, another pursuit, and something else to challenge us . . . to change what we knew and require us to think anew in order to find better answers. As long as the heart beats, this process continues. I just hope and pray that I'm doing it right.

"It's silly not to hope. It's a sin, he thought."

~ Ernest Hemingway, *The Old Man and the Sea*

In all my years, loving and helping others has never proven to be the wrong answer. At the very least, it's good to claim that powerful, unalterable truth. Maybe we couldn't truly comprehend bigger answers, those "which could not be given to you now, because you would not be able to live them," as Rilke wrote. Loving the questions and living while I am still alive . . . right here at the intersection of where I once was and what I am now, I must still make choices about who I will become. I don't know which way to go sometimes, or why things are the way they are, so I listen carefully to people, to books, and to the trees for their still, small voices. I feel a poet's voice softly moving through all the branches of myself. I kneel like T.S. Eliot, "where prayer has been valid." I ask for guidance as I faithfully search for faith itself. I look into the empty space at all my doubts and fears. I reach in carefully and put my finger right on the steady pulse of hope.

James Still, Award-winning American Playwright

Epilogue

*M*aybe you have just finished Dr. Reed's book. Maybe, like me, his book has taken you into a quiet place of reflection, a kind of twilight—not dark or light, but something in-between. If (as T.S. Eliot suggested) the ending is also the beginning, then this moment of having finished reading Dr. Reed's thoughtful and beautiful book is an ending that is a beginning, too. There is something about Dr. Reed's life (and the way he writes about it) that creates an opportunity for all of us to reflect on our own lives. It's an invitation disguised as a quiet challenge.

From the first line of the Prologue that begins, "I don't know how many hearts I've put together or replaced, well over ten thousand," I found myself admiring William Reed the pioneering heart surgeon. When Chapter One begins, "The first poets I admired were the trees," I understood that William Reed was a poet himself long before he was ever a doctor. Did the poet make him a better doctor? Did the doctor make him a better poet? And what did both of those gifts lend to his decision to write a book about his life? That is the mysterious tension that steadily illuminates Dr. Reed's memoir.

His is the story of a kid born into harsh poverty who grows up to be a renowned doctor. He was respected by colleagues for the work he did. He was loved by patients for the lives he saved. One of those lives Dr. Reed saved was mine. I was sixteen months old, it was early November, 1960. John F. Kennedy would be elected president in a few days. My parents were in their early twenties and spent hours in a waiting room at KU Medical Center. And I was on an operating table where a young doctor performed an esophageal reconstruction on me — a procedure he'd never done, never seen anyone else do; he had read about it in a book and determined it was my only chance of survival. Flash forward fifty Thanksgivings to 2009. Every Thanksgiving I thought about the doctor who saved my life, performing a new (at that time) and unusual surgery that turned out to be a great success. Starting with being alive, I had many things to be thankful for but on that particular Thanksgiving I became intent on thanking the surgeon I knew only by name and that name was Dr. William Reed. I had no memory of his face or his voice, but sometimes I would dream about his hands. I wondered if he knew I was still alive? And I wondered if he was still alive? On that particular Thanksgiving, I suddenly wanted more than anything to find Dr. Reed and tell him . . . what? It was simple and complicated. On the one hand I wanted to simply tell him thank you, thank you for saving my life. And on the other hand I wanted, strangely, to let him know that his efforts had been worth it, that I had grown up to become someone who was passionate about life, who had great capacity to love, that I was a writer deeply engaged with my work, and that I was somehow proof that everyone we touch is connected to everyone THEY touch. Everything matters. In some profound way I wanted Dr. Reed to know HIS life mattered. Thinking back on that now, and especially after reading his book I realize there was a naive arrogance in my Thanksgiving wish because I am but one of thousands whom Dr. Reed has touched.

So of course I Googled "Dr. William Reed" and quickly I fell into the internet labyrinth that led me to an email address of someone who worked in the communications department at KU Medical Center. I sent an email, explained that I was trying to find Dr. Reed . . . asked if they would pass along my information. And then a few days later—presto—I received an email from "Bill Reed" in which he wrote:

> *I received your e-mail today and I was delighted to hear from you. I remember your operation and the fact that it was the first time the procedure had been done in our region. Kind of like a surgeon's opening night, as I am sure you would appreciate as a writer.*
>
> *The number one reward throughout my career has been to feel as if I may have contributed to the joy in someone's life. It's a bit part in someone's life but essential to the big picture. Thank you for sending your note.*
>
> *Congratulations to you for all you have accomplished. I am sure that following one's passion is the secret to fulfilling one's dreams and that passion can endure.*
>
> *Please let me know if I can help you in any way. Stay in touch.*

I remember reading that email and shaking with joy. It was a completed circle somehow; but what about that sentence, "Please let me know if I can help you in any way." This man had literally saved my life! Shouldn't it have read, "Please let me know if I can help you AGAIN in any way?!!?" I noted his generous spirit. We emailed back and forth many times, sharing details about our lives, discovering the many ways we are connected. Never mind that his father's name was James and his brother was named Jimmy. Or that we were both paperboys. Or that he had grown up in Indiana and one of my most important artistic relationships is with Indiana Repertory Theatre where I've been the Playwright in Residence since 1998, commuting to Indianapolis every month from my home in Los Angeles. All of those connections . . . the ways our lives overlapped made sense in a funny way. I noted the profound difference between synchronicity and coincidence. What surprised me, however, was discovering that Dr. Reed is a lifelong student of the great poets. He freely quotes Eliot and Emerson and Yeats and Pascal and Goethe and Wordsworth. I get the feeling it isn't just the words but the ways the words make meaning that brings him back to the poems again and again. His love of language surprised me. But then again, there is something deeply economical about poetry. And intentional. And that leads me to what I find so moving about Dr. Reed — that he has lived an intentional life. There is a sense of service in Dr. Reed's medical career, service done with great compassion and humility. He never seems to have forgotten where he came from—which connects him to Eliot's poetry, too. I'm struck by the gratitude he feels for people in his life—from his mother to his first best friend to his high school machine shop teacher and especially his wife, Mary, who has been a loving life-long partner.

Reading Dr. Reed's book, I find myself engaged again and again by his thoughtfulness. I don't mean in terms of being polite or modest (although he's both of those things) but more that he is a thinking man, a man who seems to have accepted the sorrow and burden of caring about meaning. Late in the book he writes, "Why couldn't I have just as easily been born a horse and spared all this thinking?" When I read that I laughed out loud because it was so true—and so disarmingly honest.

It takes guts to write a book about your life, to risk revisiting events difficult and joyful, to dance with time itself. Knowing Dr. Reed a little bit now, his courage doesn't surprise me. I know this for sure: I'm deeply happy that the doctor who saved my life is also a poet. I love knowing that he always carried a book of poetry in his brief case. Maybe something passed between us on that operating table in 1960, maybe the prayer he said before my surgery was also a poem (and maybe they're the same thing). And maybe my own life then is a kind of poem, too. It seems to me that that's part of what Dr.

Reed has written about—the ways in which life is poetry, and poetry is an attempt to help us understand what's inside our hearts. Which brings me full circle because is it any wonder then that Dr. Reed the poet is also Dr. Reed the heart surgeon?

~ *James Still*

American author and playwright, three-time Pulitzer Prize nominee Los Angeles, California

1927 Born July 18 to William Franklin Reed and Aldine Caroline Little Reed, in rural Kokomo, Indiana

1945 Graduated Kokomo High School

Enlisted in the US Navy (became Motor Machinist Mate, Third Class)

1946 Honorably Discharged, US Navy

Enrolled at Indiana University Extension Center

1950 Graduated with a Bachelor's in Chemistry, Indiana University

Began medical school at Indiana University

1952 Met Mary Josephine Shear

1954 Graduated, M.D. from Indiana University School of Medicine

Married Mary Shear, April 4, Indianapolis, Indiana

Trained/Internship, University of Kansas Medical Center (to 1955)

1955 Did Residency, General Surgery, KUMC (to 1959)

1959 Did Residency, Thoracic Surgery, University of Kansas Medical Center (to 1960)

Received Clinical Fellowship, American Cancer Society

Received Murdock Scholarship in Medical Science;

Awarded Markel Award for Outstanding House Officer (KUMC Medical School)

1960 Given, Special Research Fellowship (National Institute of Health)

Certified, American Board of Surgery and American Board of Thoracic Surgery; Named, Associate in Surgery, KUMC

Awarded Markel Award for Outstanding House Officer (KUMC Medical School)

1961 Jeffrey Howard Reed is born on May 21

Became Associate Professor, Surgery, KUMC (to 1970)

1963 Bryan Allen Reed is born on February 5

1964 William Martin Reed is born on August 19

1970 Named Professor of Surgery & Head of Division of Thoracic Surgery, KUMC

1971 Established and became President, Mid America Thoracic & Cardiovascular Surgeons, Inc.

Named Clinical Professor of Surgery & Program Director of Thoracic Surgery, St. Luke's Hospital

Initiated Cardiothoracic Surgery Residency Training Program and served as its Director (until 1986)

Named Director of Cardiovascular Surgery, St. Luke's Hospital (through 2000)

1973 Created a Presbyterian Benevolence Fund at Second Presbyterian Church, Kansas City

Endowed a Pastor's Renewal Fund, Second Presbyterian Church, Kansas City

1975	Named Deacon, Second Presbyterian Church, Kansas City, Missouri (through 1990)
	Created Award for Teaching Excellence, Pembroke Country Day School (given annually)
	Spearheaded the development of a center focused on heart health at St. Luke's hospital (with Dr. Ben McAllister)
1977	Established The Mary Reed Award in Nursing Care, St. Luke's Hospital (financial awards given annually)
1980	Dedicated the Mid America Heart Institute at St. Luke's Hospital
1981	Named Chair, Department of Cardiovascular Diseases, St. Luke's Hospital (to 1982)

1982	Created Deer Real Estate to purchase and manage a safe, affordable apartment housing complex near KUMC for medical students, residents in training, as well as the general public
1984	Underwent heart surgery (by-pass)
	Contributed to The Williams Fund at the University of Kansas supporting athletic scholarships
1985	Initiated Heart Transplant Program at St. Luke's Hospital
	Performed the first heart transplant at St. Luke's Hospital
1988	Named Medical Director, Cardiovascular Surgery Program, St. Luke's Hospital

continued

Transplanting hope

Reeds pledge $1.5M to begin developing heart transplant program

Cardiac surgery pioneer William Reed, MD, and his wife, Mary, have hearts of gold when it comes to supporting and expanding heart care at The University of Kansas Hospital.

In April, the hospital announced its commitment to develop a heart transplant program as part of a comprehensive heart failure center. At the same time, the Reeds announced their pledge of $1.5 million to help

1991	Bought land and built Heartland Farm, a Kentucky-style horse farm in the countryside south of Kansas City, Missouri
1992	Horseracing begins in earnest
1994	Formed Stonecrest Farm Thoroughbred Breeding and Racing (originally Heartland Farm begun in 1991)
1999	Created **The Reed Family Foundation**, a non-profit supporting charitable causes. Perfect Drift is born at Wayfare Farm in Lexington, Kentucky, in April Diagnosed with prostate cancer Led the rebuilding of the cardiovascular program at the University of Kansas Medical Center (with Dr. Steve Owens)
2000	Named Director of Cardiac Surgery, Clinical Professor of Surgery, University of Kansas Medical Center
2001	Established The Outstanding Nursing Award at the University of Kansas Hospital
2002	Hosted Summer Youth Horse Camp at Stonecrest Farm for youth including underprivileged children
2002	Retired from operating after over ten thousand open-heart surgeries and another two thousand surgical heart procedures Perfect Drift places third in the Kentucky Derby in May

The Reed Family Foundation
supports:

Armed Services Aid

Barstow School

Boys & Girls Club

Center for Advanced Heart Care at the University of Kansas Hospital

*Friendship Inn
(a temporary housing facility for families with hospitalized patients)*

Girl Scouts

Great Plains ASPCA

Harvesters Community Food Network

Help Me See Foundation

Help Our Wounded Veterans

Hospital Veterans

Indiana University

Kansas City Mounted Patrol

Kansas City Public Library

Kansas City Union Mission

Kansas University Endowment Association

National Blind Veterans

National Federation for the Blind

Padre Pio Academy

Paralyzed Veterans

Police Family Survivors Fund

United Service Organizations

Urban League

World War II Veterans

2003	Tested for MDS (slow progression of myelodysplastic syndrome; confirmed diagnosis in 2014)		Reed Cardiovascular Surgery Center there in their honor
			Raced for the fifth (and last) time in The Breeder's Cup, Perfect Drift set the record for most times qualified to run in this, the world's most prestigious horse race
2003 - 2012	Established The Mary Reed Equine Compassion Fund, Kansas State University Foundation (awarded annually to a veterinary resident in training)		
			Proven Cure won the LittleBitLively Stake at Remington Park in Oklahoma, and became only the fifth thoroughbred since 1976 to win a stakes race at the age of twelve
	Faculty Support Fund, Veterinary Medicine, Clinical Sciences, Kansas State University		
	The Miles Fund, Veterinary Medical Teaching Hospital, Kansas State University	2007	Awarded Lifetime Service Award & Heroes in Healthcare by Ingram's Magazine
	Funded, Equine Departmental Support, Kansas State University		

> *"No matter what he professes to be his religious belief,*
> *the best indication of what a man stands for*
> *is how he uses the gifts he's been given."*
>
> ~ William A. Reed

2004	Mary Reed established a non-profit foundation supporting the Kansas City Mounted Patrol (with Sgt. Kim Hannon and Mary Ellen Puruker); The Reeds contribute funds and equipment, host fundraisers, and have donated horses.	2008	Contributed to The Pat Day Fund in support of the racetrack backside people (an on-going donation)
			Endowed a Pastor's Fund at the Church of the Resurrection, Overland Park, Kansas
	Contributed $1 million dollars to support the construction of the heart hospital at KUMC		
2006	Dedicated the Heart Hospital at KUMC; the University of Kansas Hospital chose to name The William and Mary	2009	Established a Million Dollar Legacy Fund for the Wesley Society at the Church of the Resurrection, Overland Park, Kansas

continued

2010   Appointed, Chairman of the
        Board of the Kansas Health
        Policy Authority (through
        2011)

2011   Created The Mary Reed
        Animal Benevolence Fund

2012   Received the Hall of Fame
        Legacy Award from the
        University of Kansas Hospital

        Gifted $1.5 million to re-
        establish the Heart Transplant
        Program, KUMC

2013   Donated $1 million dollars
        to the capital campaign
        building fund, Church of the
        Resurrection, Overland Park,
        Kansas

2014   Pledged $450,000 to
        the creation of a non-
        denominational meditation
        chapel at KUMC

        Received the Lifetime
        Achievement Award from the
        Metropolitan Medical Society
        of Kansas City

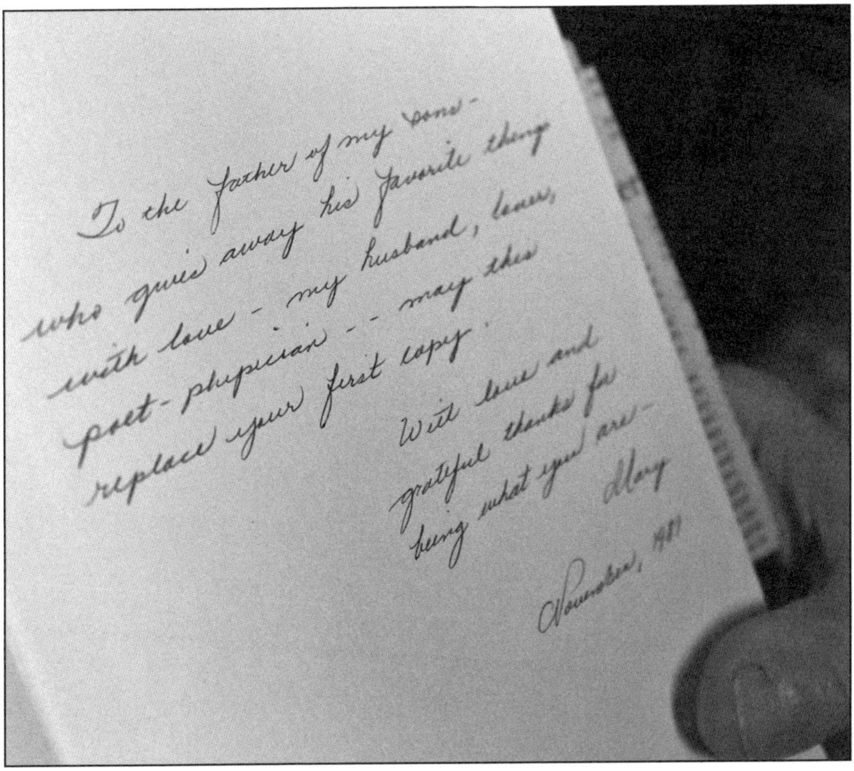

"None of this was possible without Mary."

~ William Reed